D1550316

Go Motorhoming
and Campervanning

I

Special Thanks: We are indebted to the following industry experts who generously gave up their time to proofread this book: Andy Clarke (www.ukmotorhomes.net), Barry Crawshaw, Barry Norris, Dave Hurrell and Gentleman Jack. Full-timers George and Kate Zekan perused and commented on the content in 2014 ensuring that this book is up to date. We are also grateful to Don Madge and the people from companies, organisations, and members of the public that helped us along the way. We are especially thankful to those people that helped to shed light on the numerous moot points discussed in this book.

Vicarious Editorial Team, Vicarious Books, 62 Tontine Street, Folkestone, Kent, CT20 1JP.
Authors: Chris Doree and Meli George
Contributing writers: Andy and Sue Glasgow
Editors: Chris Doree and Meli George
Editorial assistants: Caroline Stacey and Sophie Bedwell
Copy editor: Pami Hoggatt
Design and artwork: Chris Gladman Design Tel: 07745 856652

Front cover main image: Arcade, Spain.

First published in Great Britain by Vicarious Books LLP, 2006. This edition published by Vicarious Media Ltd 2015.
© Vicarious Media 2015.
Copyright © text Vicarious Media.
Copyright © photographs Vicarious Media unless otherwise stated.
ISBN: 978-1-910664-02-5

CONTENTS

Go Motorhoming and Campervanning

What is a motorhome: a car, a house, an escape? No wonder you've always wanted one. Whether it is the retirement present you have worked so hard for or a cheap campervan to go on tour, you will love it just the same.

Throughout this book we use the umbrella term 'motorhome' regardless of vehicle size and origin. Therefore campervans, mobile-homes, motor caravans, recreational vehicles (RVs), and camping cars are all 'motorhomes'.

Motorhomes make perfect transport to see the sights or enjoy Mediterranean winters. They can help you find a new life abroad, and they enable thousands of hobbyists to follow their passion.

Go Motorhoming is not a fluffy travelogue, but a fact-packed, no-nonsense guide that will turn a novice into a pro. Even the most experienced motorhomer will be inspired to make more of their foreign escapades.

Whatever your calling, your motorhome offers you freedom and spontaneity unrivalled by any other means of travel, always with that home from home feeling, wherever you find yourself.

Go Motorhoming and Campervanning

La Suze sur Sarthe, France.

Mosel Valley, Germany.

CHAPTER 1 - Understanding Motorhoming

Do people buy motorhomes to go 'motorhoming' or to pursue their interests? Do you know where you want to go, how often and for how long? Why choose a motorhome over a caravan? Perhaps you are reading this book to answer these questions. Read through to the summary and you will know the answers to all these questions and many more, as well as gaining a complete understanding of motorhoming.

Caravans outnumber motorhomes in the UK because most UK campsites are found in rural locations, thus a mode of transport is beneficial and none is more convenient than the car that towed the caravan. Having to decamp your pitch and prepare your motorhome for the road so that you can drive to the local shops or attractions soon becomes a chore. Most British caravan owners restrict their travels to 50 miles from home and few take their caravans abroad, but those that do tend to stop on one campsite for the majority of their holiday. Restrictive UK regulations force the majority of campers to stay at official campsites, making a car and caravan more practical than a motorhome. The tables turn as soon as you decide that you mostly want to travel on the Continent because many European countries permit the occupants of a motorised vehicle to cook, eat and sleep 'within' the vehicle when parked. DVLA (Driver Vehicle Licensing Agency) registers motorhomes by the old fashioned name, Motor Caravan, which by design is a personal motorised vehicle with self-sufficient accommodation (see page 56 for more detail). Caravans are temporary static accommodation with wheels for transportation, and using them is deemed as camping which may only be done at campsites.

Caravans outnumber motorhomes in the UK.

There are approximately 10,000 motorhome stopovers across Europe. Sancoins, France.

Throughout this book we refer to stopping overnight by the side of the road as Offsite-Parking. Over the decades Offsite-Parking has developed in such a way that officially designated motorhome parking places, referred to as Motorhome Stopovers in this book, are very common in: France (Aires), Germany (Stellplätze) and Italy (Sosta). Motorhome Stopovers are mostly located in towns and villages, but are also by the coast, alongside rivers and canals, and at ski resorts. The majority of Motorhome Stopovers are simple car parks without a reception or guardian, but most have Service Points where toilet cassettes can be emptied and fresh water drawn. Often both the parking and service is free. The expectation is that motorhomers will spend their money locally and stop for no more than two nights. This unencumbered, come-and-go-as-you-please system is so popular in Europe that motorhomers use Motorhome Stopovers far more than campsites. Chapter 6 fully discusses accommodation options.

Chinese whispers are rife in the motorhoming and caravanning community, so there are plenty of rumours going around and some are so old that they are practically biblical. Over the past 13 years we have spent more than 1,000 nights parked offsite all over Europe without incident. The biggest concern amongst inexperienced motorhomers is being gassed and broken into at Motorhome Stopovers. The College of Anaesthetists has stated in

Motorhome Stopovers often have a drinking water tap and somewhere to empty your toilet.

writing that it is not possible to render someone unconscious in a motorhome; see their statement on page 95. At the time of publishing there was no official record of gas being used during burglary. If you are still unconvinced, research the siege of the Russian Dubrovka Theatre on 23rd October 2002. Unfortunately, motorhomes, caravans, cars, trucks, and coaches do get broken into at motorway service and rest areas, especially in southern France and Spain.

No wonder Motorhome Stopovers are very popular in Europe. Plougasnou, France.

French motorway services are also called Aires.

The French word Aire translates to area. Confusingly, both motorway rest areas and designated Motorhome Stopovers are commonly referred to and named 'Aires' in France. Motorhome break ins have frequently been incorrectly reported and until recently the fact that the victims were parked at motorway service areas, not official Motorhome Stopovers, has not been clarified. Be vigilant at all times when using motorway rest and service areas, and never park overnight even if it has a motorhome Service Point.

Having decided that you want to tour without constraint, rather than book in and set up on campsites, you can consider yourself a motorhomer. As you travel from place to place, you pick up everything you need to allow you to park for a few days. You then explore the local area on foot, by pushbike or by public transport, so an additional engine-driven mode of transport is unnecessary. If you are adamant that you are only going to stop at campsites, then you can consider yourself a camper. The good news is that a car and caravan/tent can be purchased significantly cheaper than a motorhome and are a much more practical option for campsite use. We realise that some people simply do not want to tow, especially a large caravan, or do not have a licence to tow their desired caravan. If you think that a caravan would be more suitable for you, consider attending one of The Caravan Club's towing courses or gain your towing licence.

Maiden Voyage

Travelling by motorhome for the first time can be a daunting experience, but if you are doing so in your own motorhome you will have already come a long way. Motorhomes are a luxury purchase and only time will tell how frequently you use one, if at all, and whether or not you made a good buying decision. Just about all

A modern VW Camper Van available for hire. www.conceptcamperhire.co.uk

motorhome owners would agree that hiring a motorhome before you buy, especially if you have not owned a touring caravan, is highly recommended. Ensure that you hire a motorhome with a toilet. Before you hire, read the small print and check what costs are incurred for damage. Are there any territorial restrictions, for example Great Britain mainland only? Australian hire companies exclude you from driving down dirt roads unless a 4x4 is hired. The handover may be basic, but ensure you understand how to turn the water and gas on and off, how to fill the water and gas tanks and how to empty the toilet and waste water. Make up the bed and make sure you know where everything is before you leave the hire company. If something breaks down or gets broken, contact the hire company immediately as they may be able to give advice and suggest where repairs can be made. Always contact the hire company before work is undertaken and keep any receipts. Do make sure you return a clean camper with empty toilet and waste tanks to avoid expensive cleaning charges.

We recommend that you take a trip to France to learn what European motorhoming has to offer. Buy and study the appropriate guidebooks in advance, as these are unlikely to be for sale at the hire depot. Stop overnight in campsites of varying standards and at Motorhome Stopovers to get the full experience.

Australian hire companies only allow their 4x4 motorhomes to be driven on dirt roads.

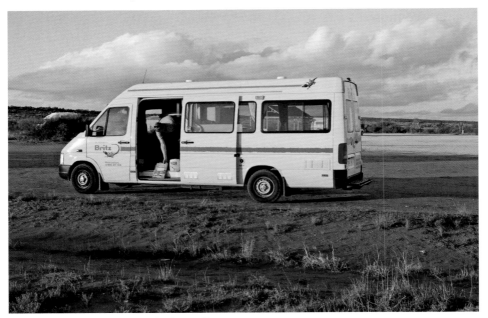

Going bush is quite normal in Australia.

We hired a motorhome in Perth, Australia. After a 20-hour flight and a couple of hours sleep at a cheap hotel, we walked to the hire company adjacent to the airport to collect our motorhome. Having completed the paperwork, we watched an induction DVD and had a very quick handover. From Perth we travelled 1,200km north to Coral Bay in Western Australia. The motorhome gave us freedom to explore anywhere accessible by asphalt road. We purchased a Camps Australia Wide, www.campsaustraliawide.com, book at a camping and outdoor shop and this gave us the locations of serviced parking areas where we could camp out in the bush. This proved to be much cheaper than doing the same trip staying in campsites or hiring a car and stopping at hotels. We saw amazing sunsets and sunrises over the Australian bush and cooked our dinner over open fires.

Hiring a motorhome might seem expensive, but doing so will almost certainly save you money in the long run. With the experience gained you are more likely to buy a compatible motorhome for your needs and intended use, rather than one that you perceived would be perfect.

Some hire companies offer special purchase deals post hire. A list of hire companies can be found at www.motorhome-list.org.uk/links.htm or check the adverts in motorhome magazines.

An equally viable option to hiring is to buy a budget motorhome that has reached the point where depreciation is entirely down to condition. Therefore, if used sympathetically for a short time there should be little difference between purchase and sale price. This is a great way to find out what you must have, but more importantly what you can do without. Buy carefully and you should have no problem reselling. See Chapter 2 for a full explanation. The success of your first trip will depend on your forward planning.

Escorted tours save you the job of planning and provide a reassuring backup. You will meet at a designated place, probably at a port, and then drive your motorhome between pre-planned destinations. You may drive in convoy or self-navigate, giving you the freedom to visit places of interest en route. The tour leaders will be experienced motorhomers as will some of the other people on tour. All will be happy to talk to you and offer help when required. Experienced motorhomers may find that organised tours provide a relaxing holiday or the opportunity to visit places they would not wish to visit alone.

We travelled with GB Privilege on an escorted holiday to the Netherlands to visit the Christmas markets in Valkenburg's caves. Included in the price of the tour were all ferry crossings, maps, campsite fees, entrance to the caves, a bus trip to a neighbouring town's market and a communal restaurant meal. We found it stress-free despite staying in a busy campsite in a hectic tourist area. We frequently met people from the tour around the town and markets, which some people found reassuring. The tour comprised first-timers and experienced motorhomers, many of whom assisted the first-timers in getting everything working and answering their questions. For more information contact GB Privilege, www.gbprivilege.com, Tel: 01273 301930.

Adventurous people may find it practical to join escorted tours when undertaking long overlanding trips. Escorted tours provide visa assistance and the necessary support you will need to complete an adventure around the Mediterranean or on the Silk Route to China. Contact Mir Tours, a German company that organises various extreme trips annually, www.mir-tours.de, Tel: 0049 6746 80280.

Mother Ivey's Bay beach and campsite are busy during the summer holidays.

School's Out For Summer

Southern Europeans traditionally take the whole of August off work, Scandinavians holiday in July and the French take holidays in both July and August. During the summer holidays campsites near the sea, and at any other tourist hotspot, can be full to capacity despite charging peak rates. Aires at holiday destinations are likely to be oversubscribed. Conversely, cities can be deserted and shops shut.

If you prefer a quieter holiday consider visiting anywhere that is not an obvious tourist destination. The authors travelled extensively around inland France throughout August 2014. Road traffic was less than normal and few campsites were more than 50 per cent occupied. Motorhome Aires were no more occupied than they would be in the spring or autumn.

Holiday makers generally return to work or school during the last week of August through to the first week of September. After the exodus campsites can take on a ghost town appearance, but most stay open until the end of September. If you have no other commitments do take advantage of the glorious September sunshine and reduced campsite rates.

Keep your cool

The landmass effect of mainland Europe causes higher summer temperatures than those experienced in Great Britain. Thus the heat may be unbearable without, and sometimes even with, air conditioning. The hottest destinations are southern Spain, Italy, and Greece.

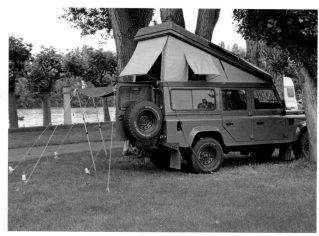

Park in the shade to keep cool during summer.

Motorhomes are normally white in colour to reduce heat gain, but strong sunshine causes internal temperatures to rise quickly heating both the fabric and contents of the motorhome. After sunset outside temperatures will fall, but the motorhome acts as a storage heater and internal temperatures can still be uncomfortable at bedtime. Simple heat management techniques can help you enjoy the sunshine without having to use air conditioning.

Always try to park in the shade taking into account where the sun will move to. The perfect pitch would have early morning and late afternoon sun, but deep shade during the day. Ideally your motorhome will be fitted with window blinds that have a silver backing to reflect the sun's rays. The cab windows cause terrific solar gain, so close curtains or blinds on these windows. Alternatively, cover the windscreen with reflective screens. Creating a through draught can be very effective at reducing heat. Unfortunately your insurance will be void if you leave windows or top vents open when the motorhome is left unattended. To escape high summer temperatures head north and high, ideally to a forested area in the mountains so that you can keep cool under the trees.

Most motorhomes are fitted with 3-way absorption fridges and these may struggle to keep contents cool in very hot conditions. To give your fridge the best chance, always park with the fridge side of the motorhome away from the sun. See page 63 for a full explanation of how 3-way absorption fridges operate.

Swimming is a great summer pastime that can provide a much needed cool down. There are excellent swimming facilities at French lakes and many of the municipal campsites are adjacent to swimmable rivers. Norwegian and Swedish fjords often have free recreational areas with facilities such as changing rooms, toilets, barbeque sites, wooden piers, and

Chris cools off in a forest pool.

diving platforms. Even high in the Arctic Circle the water can be warm. Italy is the worst place to go for a beach holiday as most of the beaches are private and only small areas are open to the public, often in the most inconvenient places. In addition to a swimming costume, take water shoes (diving suit material with rubber soles) which are available at most seaside towns. Consider taking a waterproof pouch if you have an electronic key fob or don't want keys to suffer water and salt corrosion.

Norway is well worth visiting in June or July as long as you have a healthy budget. Temperatures are similar to the UK with the rain to match, so avoid Scandinavia if forecasters predict a wet summer. If you are lucky and visit during a heat wave, you will be able to make the most of the Arctic Circle's pristine beaches. Minor motorhome modifications may be necessary, firstly to protect you from the ever-present mosquitoes and secondly to ensure internal darkness as 24-hour daylight plays

Norway is a fantastic location even at midnight. Photo: Andy Glasgow.

havoc with natural sleep patterns. People are often out of bed in the middle of the night, so avoid pitching near communal areas as these can be noisy.

Who turned out the Northern Lights? Unfortunately the Aurora Borealis is not visible during the summer and during the winter the Arctic Circle is too cold and icy for motorhome travel.

Winter Sun-Seekers

The phrase 'sun-seeker' refers to motorhomers and caravanners who migrate south for the winter. The peak period for winter sun-seeking is January to March, but some people start heading south in October. What could be nicer than slowly meandering south in 25°C daytime temperatures, stopping off at deserted beaches whilst the seas are still warm, and witnessing the grape, olive and citrus fruits harvests? Sun-seekers then return to northerly countries in the spring before southern temperatures become unbearable and the busy tourist season begins. Many winter sun-seekers have proven that Spain can be driven to in a couple of long days, but you will need to drive fast and follow the main roads and motorways. We think this is balmy. Why exhaust yourself when you can drive the scenic route and start your holiday from Calais?

Chantada wine region in Spain could be visited on your way south.

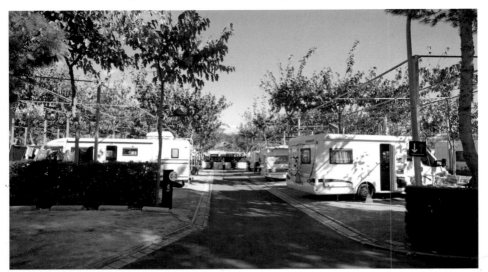

Camping Bonterra Park, in Spain, is located in the town and near the beach.

Campsites usually cater very well for the long-stay winter visitor with some sites offering regular events, activities, and transport to the local town or bus/train station. Many campers return year after year, forming strong communities which could be collectively described as a gossip. Campsite location is very important. Ideally there should be good public transport links and the option to walk to a town or vibrant village from the campsite. Advance booking will be necessary at well-located campsites.

Southern Spain is the warmest European location in the depths of winter and the coastal campsites can be full. Most days will be warm enough for you to be comfortable wearing shorts. On sunny days you will be able to sit outside and top up your tan, but it will be cool in the shade and the sea. Expect coastal Spain to be busy. There will be plenty of British company and there are many places to spend your euros, but be vigilant as handbag snatching and pickpocketing is not uncommon in Spain. Christmas to the end of February is peak season and reserving a pitch may not be possible, especially if you have a very large motorhome. Municipal Motorhome Stopovers are few and far between in southern Spain. As a result privately run Stopovers are popping up all over the place; often these Stopovers have campsite licences. Crowding is not exclusive to Spanish campsites, the Offsite-Parking fraternity also complain that it is difficult to find overnight parking during the winter months. Pre-recession development of the Spanish coast has removed many popular spots and put pressure on

Popular campsites, like Camping la Manga, will be very busy during winter.

the places that remain. Unfortunately, some people abuse the goodwill of locals by staying weeks on end or, worse still, camping rather than parking.

Winter campsites are among the few places at which you might see an American-style articulated pickup truck and trailer, known as a fifth wheel, or large American-style motorhomes, known as RVs. These large units provide comfortable living space, air conditioning, and large under-floor lockers. If you intend to buy a large fifth wheel or a large motorhome, read Chapter 6 carefully as many campsites cannot accommodate large units. Also, fifth wheels are classed as caravans so are not allowed at Motorhome Stopovers.

Consider renting a season pitch if you intend to stay on a campsite longer than a few months. Some campsites offer pitches on a 99-year lease, www.caravanrentallamanga.com. Wintering in Spain is so popular that many clubs organise annual winter rallies to Spain. People find this convenient as their pitches are reserved for them and there are trips and activities organised during their stay. A rally tent provides a meeting place and information point and there is likely to be a book swap box. Contact The Caravan Club, www.caravanclub.co.uk, The Camping and Caravanning Club, www.campingandcaravanningclub.co.uk or The Motor Caravanners' Club, www.motorcaravanners.eu, and enquire about their winter rally programmes.

Go Motorhoming and Campervanning

The biggest advantage of heading to Spain, aside from the warmth, is that two other countries, Portugal and Morocco, can easily be visited as part of your winter sun tour. Portugal is slightly cooler than Spain, but has far more charm. The overall situation is similar to Spain and most motorhomes congregate in the Algarve as this is the warmest area. Motorhome Stopovers are generally located inland or on the cooler Atlantic coast. Even though Portugal's coast is much less developed than Spain's, regular Offsite-Parkers have complained that many communal water taps have been turned off and previous parking areas have been blocked off.

Morocco is the warmest and cheapest easily accessible winter destination off the Continent and grows in popularity every year. During the winter, around 100 campsites stay open and there are some Offsite-Parking opportunities. Morocco maintains a strong North African identity making it an interesting place to visit. People that have not been to Morocco may feel it is unsafe, but this is unjustified. Crime against tourists is rare because of the harsh penalties. In reality you are far more likely to be a victim of crime in Spain.

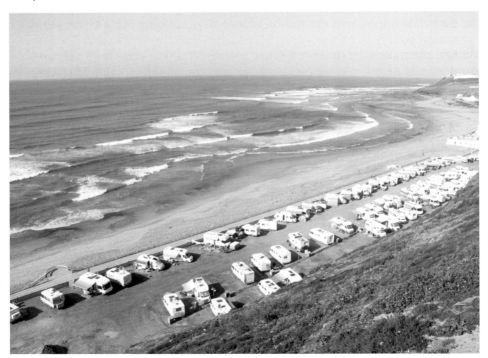

Morocco is warmer than Spain during winter. Camping El Barco. Photo: Andy Clarke.

Morocco does offer an off-the-beaten-track destination, but Offsite-Parking is now discouraged. Hundreds of motorhomes once Offsite-Parked unrestricted at Banana Beach. Now guardians take nightly fees and the authorities keep a close eye on things. There is plenty of guarded parking in Morocco, but this is no guarantee that you are allowed to park overnight or that the guardian will guard the vehicle. If you intend to visit Morocco, read *Camping Morocco* by Vicarious Books. If you do not want to travel to Morocco independently, then GB Privilege can escort you.

Other winter sun destinations include Sicily, Greece, and Turkey. Sicily, and to a lesser degree southern Italy, provide some camping and Offsite-Parking opportunities, but the winter temperatures are normally a couple of degrees cooler than southern Spain. You can expect to find fewer than 100 motorhomes touring Sicily during the winter. The facilities are very limited and you have to be prepared to be self-sufficient.

Greece is cooler and much quieter than Spain during the winter. You have to take a ferry from Italy to Greece unless you drive the long way around the Adriatic, but this drive is best saved for the spring. Few motorhomers, and even fewer caravanners, make it to Greece, so do not be surprised if you are on your own most of the time. Offsite-Parking is illegal in Greece and few campsites are open during the winter, but the ones that are open are often inexpensive and quiet.

Standard winter daylight saving does not suit us, so we set our clocks forward an hour when we are on the Continent and two when in Greece. This encourages us to go to bed earlier and naturally wake up earlier, therefore we make the most of the limited daylight. There are spin-offs to this time management because you use less battery power when not on hook-up and you can depart earlier so you get to tourist sites or campsites before they become busy.

Turkey is considered a far-flung motorhome destination, but it is a great place to visit during the winter months. You will experience higher temperatures than in mainland Europe and a different culture. There are campsites open in winter, but, just as in Greece, expect to be on your own most of the time.

The rain will fall in Spain and there is a possibility of snow and frost. After Christmas most people will consider the sea too cold for swimming. Consider visiting Australia and New Zealand for guaranteed winter sun.

Go Motorhoming and Campervanning

Wave, Wind, And Snow

Motorhomes are popular with sea and mountain sports enthusiasts who chase wind or snow to engage in their sport with optimal conditions. Menageries of motorhomes collect in little groups at secret surf spots all around Europe – testament to the cheap and convenient accommodation these vehicles provide. Heavy

Surf vans in Spain.

equipment could be a problem, so ensure you read Chapter 2 as many motorhomes have sufficient weight capacity for passengers and limited luggage only.

Winter sports enthusiasts should purchase a motorhome designed to cope with very low temperatures. Ski resorts often have high altitude campsites and Motorhome Stopovers, so sub-zero temperatures are to be expected. During January and February temperatures will be around -15°C at night, though -21°C is not unusual. Motorhoming in freezing conditions is discussed at length in Chapter 4.

Camping near the ski slopes at Grimentz. Photo: Andy Glasgow.

Motorhome loaded with leisure equipment.

Brissac Quince Château, France.

Valencia de Don Juan, Spain.

The Grand Tour

There are other ways to tour Europe, but none is as convenient or as effective as touring by motorhome. You have total independence and the only restrictions will be self-imposed. £1,000 per month is sufficient for two people touring in a motorhome, just £16 each per day! People on tour mostly use Motorhome Stopovers where parking is often restricted to 48 hours. Not all towns have a Motorhome Stopover, so using these will mean you naturally deviate off the tourist trail.

Following an itinerary helps provide structure to your journey, but often your best memories are not Florence, Rome or Paris but the sleepy town where you drank with the locals. Read a general guide to Europe in advance as this will highlight the best bits and give you an idea of where you want to spend your time. You could easily spend a year discovering France, Germany, or Italy and guidebooks are essential to help you choose where to go and what to see. Several books provide information on the traditional Grand Tour, including Kevin McCloud's *Grand Tour of Europe* and Brian Sewell's *Grand Tour*. Literary reads include *Little Dorrit* by Charles Dickens and *A Room With A View* by E M Forster.

Neuschwanstein Castle, Bavaria.

Overlanding

Driving around Europe is not extreme enough to be considered overlanding. European motorhomes are not designed for real overlanding, so people convert all-wheel drive vehicles (4x4s) to include living accommodation. Popular overlanding tours include the old trade routes through Asia and Africa.

X-Cap French manufacturer, www.3ccartier.com.

Europe is a good place to start your overlanding adventure as you can drive to the Middle East and Asia or head south and across to Africa. This book details everything you need to know about motorhoming in Europe, but also read *The Overlanders' Handbook* by Chris Scott. Also visit the following websites: The Silk Route Motorcaravan Network, www.silkroute.org.uk, www.xor.org.uk and www.go-overland.com. Mir Tours, a German company, leads various overlanding trips, visit www.mir-tours.de, Tel: 0049 6746 80280.

Morocco could be the start of your overland adventure. Photo: Andy Clarke.

Full-Timing

Full-Timing is the term used to describe people that live solely in their motorhome. Having prepared your motorhome, yourself, and your affairs, you are set free like a fledgling bird. Ask yourself: How are you going to occupy your time when you have no work or family commitments and no social engagements? Where are you going to go? Europe seems very small when you consider that trucks trundle from Calais to the furthest points of Europe within a working week. The perception of Full-Timing is a highly romanticised alternative way of living. The reality is that few people live full-time in their motorhomes because alternative lifestyles only suit a minority of people. Motorhomes by design are touring vehicles and medium-sized motorhomes are the best compromise between drivability and home comfort when touring. When you live full-time in a motorhome, you need space and storage and that means you need something the size of a coach. Unfortunately, Europe is not set up for coach-sized motorhomes and therefore you have to plan every move. Ask yourself, do you want to live in a motorhome or do you want to use a motorhome so that you can see the sights?

We gave up our careers and set off full-time for as long as our budget allowed. In the first 10 months, we clocked up 27,000 miles through 15 countries as we toured to the four compass points of Europe. Long-term touring is demanding, both mentally and physically, and we were exhausted after our whistle-stop tour of Europe. We moved much slower for the next two years and changed from a motorhome to a touring caravan, and then to holiday accommodation. We have learnt that four months is our limit before we need a break from touring.

Most Full-Timers take extended periods of campsite recuperation, normally through the winter. Some escape their motorhomes and go travelling in other parts of the world or spend some time on organised activities. We recommend that you consider Full-Timing for a year or so, rather than for the rest of your life. If you own property, we urge you to keep somewhere to return to, even if you have to down-size to release capital. Property that is easy to rent is best as the rent will help fund your trip or pay for repairs and redecoration upon your return.

Isolation can be a problem for all travellers and motorhomers on tour may go for weeks without having a decent conversation. Travelling alone is hard,

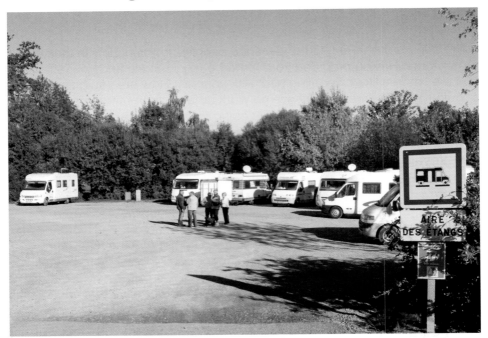

A gossip of motorhomers share information.

but even people travelling as a couple suffer isolation; after all, you know everything the other person has done. You will quickly spot sufferers as they tend to jump out of their motorhome, no matter how bad the weather, eager to speak to anyone with a British number plate. Presumably this happens to other nationalities because in remote places everyone appears to be the best of friends. Sufferers have to talk at you for around ten minutes with tales of great finds and breakdowns before they are capable of a two-way conversation. To help keep isolation at bay it is good to socialise and swap information whenever possible, be it with the locals or other campers. Even without foreign language skills, with a little effort you can still have some good times and excellent experiences with the natives or other nationalities. Try to say something in their language even if it is only 'hello' ('hallo' in German). Spontaneous evenings can be great fun and what you learn may set you off in a new direction. All you need is a bottle and some 'bottle' – thankfully one normally brings the other. Non-drinkers will find having a book to swap or any other spurious excuse like "I don't suppose you have a widget like this one" also works well. Most people are happy to chat whether they are touring or static. The very least you should do is let your neighbouring motorhomers know who is in your motorhome as they may act as your security. Sometimes a simple wave from an oncoming British motorhome is exciting. Identifying number plates is hard and it would be much nicer if everybody had a GB sticker on the front, as well as the back, of the motorhome. Chances are you will end up bumping into some motorhomers again and again.

Bon Voyage

Whatever type of motorhomer you are, the important thing is to go. There is never a right time and you never know what will happen in the future. Should you discover that you do not like motorhoming, at least you have tried. And if you love it, the quicker you go the better.

Ferries leaving Dover for the Continent.

Vicarious Shop

- Details over 99 per cent of France's Aires
- Inspected and photographed Aires
- Easy directions, On-site GPS co-ordinates
- LPG stations
- Aires for big motorhomes

Motorhomes have the privilege of staying on Motorhome Stopovers, known as Aires. Information about these can be found on page 180.

CHAPTER 2 - Your Motorhome

Dr Who's Tardis is the ultimate motorhome, a go-anywhere vehicle with every creature comfort, but it is presently unavailable! Earth-based motorhome manufacturers have to work within the constraints of three dimensions, but are currently offering over 1,000 new models. When you consider that motorhomes have a 90-year history there is a bewildering selection of makes and models. DVLA register about 9,000 new motorhomes per year in Great Britain. On the 30th September 2014 there were 230,768 taxed motorhomes and 31,277 SORN.

Motorhomes for sale at an outdoor motorhome show.

Getting To Know Motorhome Types

Most motorhomes are built upon or utilise some or all of a light commercial vehicle. Fiat's Ducato has been the dominant base vehicle in recent years, but its siblings Citroën Relay and Peugeot Boxer are also used. All three brands are manufactured in the same SEVEL factory in Italy. Other makes include Mercedes Sprinter, Ford Transit, Iveco Daily, VW Transporter and Renault Master. Fiat and Ford produce special low and wide-track motorhome chassis that offer enhanced ride and handling. Their design means the caravan body floor is closer to the ground. Some motorhomes have AL-KO galvanised chassis that provide similar attributes, but they also have independent torsion suspension.

AL-KO chassis cowl.

Most modern motorhomes have a diesel engine as standard, but older and smaller motorhomes and American RVs may be petrol driven. Diesel engines offer high torque at low revs making them the most suitable for heavy motorhomes. Also, diesel is often considerably cheaper than unleaded petrol in Europe, so it is worth choosing a diesel engine. Leaded petrol is not widely available on the Continent, but the lead substitute added to unleaded fuel is. LPG is available on the Continent, but not widely in every country. See Chapter 3 for LPG fuel station locations.

Left to right: Low-profile Coachbuilt, Panel Van Conversion (PVC), and A-Class motorhome.

There are three distinct motorhome types: Van Conversions, Coachbuilt, and A-Class. 'White-Van Man' can deliver anywhere and manoeuvrability is what makes Van Conversions so practical. Coachbuilt motorhomes are the most common conversion and offer the best value for money. A-Class motorhomes are the cream of the crop and can cost as much as a house.

Van Conversions are converted panel vans, sometimes referred to as PVCs. Modern vans have a car-like drive and, despite

Bailey Approach Coachbuilt with overcab bed.

VW Van Conversion being manufactured at Concept Multi Car Ltd.

modest proportions, many Van Conversions are practical for long-term touring. Converters adapt everything from car-derived vans right up to the biggest Mercedes and Iveco high cube monsters. Ignoring length, panel vans have less internal space than Coachbuilt and A-Class motorhomes for two reasons. Coachbuilt and A-Class motorhomes have upright sidewalls, but panel van sidewalls slope inwards slightly. Coachbuilt and A-Class motorhomes are generally 2.3m (7'7") wide, but a panel van is 2m (6'7") wide or less. Converting a panel van is awkward because most of the work has to be done within the confines of the van. This is time consuming and therefore increases the conversion cost. Van Conversions sold well during the recession, partly due to low prices but mainly because of the increased width of modern vans. 2m-wide vans can have widthways beds long enough to be comfortable for people up to 1.83m (6') tall. Transverse beds across the back of the van are popular and functional. Often there is a large storage space under the bed or it folds up creating a walkway through the middle. This makes it possible to load bikes or even sheets of plywood for a DIY project.

Left: *This Auto Campers Day Van 3 can be used as a van and a camper.*
www.auto-campers.co.uk
Right: *A 1980s Hymer A-Class and a 2008 Pilote A-Class.*

The open sliding door provides a place to sit and enjoy the view. Chris enjoys a view of Western Australia.

Big sliding side doors really connect you to the outside world when parked up, although sometimes too much when it is cold or raining.

There is nothing nicer than sitting comfortably inside your van looking out over a great view. Unfortunately, many Van Conversions have a kitchen in the sliding doorway spoiling this fantastic attribute. Consider others when opening and closing sliding doors during the night because they are noisy no matter how careful you are. If you feel comfortable with the internal space offered in a Van Conversion, we recommend that you buy one.

Smaller Van Conversions, including the iconic VW camper, are called Campervans and Day Vans. Some modern Campervans have a high top roof, but elevating roofs (pop-tops) are more common. Material sides protect you from wind and rain, but they offer little physical security. Campervans are the cool, small, camping tool. These smaller vehicles are often used as daily transport, but the constrained proportions dictate that facilities

Campingplatz Halbinsel Burg, Lake Staffelsee, Bavaria.

have to be small and are often very basic. Showers are rarely installed, so a separate toilet cubicle is unlikely. Refrigeration will be limited or non-existent. These factors mean that Campervans are rarely self-sufficient and therefore not suitable for Offsite-Parking. Campervans work best for day visits to the beach or a bed for the night when staying out late and they

Assorted campernalia and additional sleeping accommodation required by these campervanners in Australia.

come into their own on a relaxed campsite where you can spread out your campernalia.

Coachbuilt motorhomes best fit the official name Motor Caravan as a caravan body is built upon a light commercial vehicle chassis and the original cab is retained. This is the least expensive way to build a motorhome as much of the conversion is completed before the sidewalls and roof are fitted. Sometimes the caravan body is mounted onto a platform cab rather than a bare chassis. Coachbuilt motorhomes often have a sleeping area over the cab and the roof profile is designed to offer internal space. Some over-cab-bed Coachbuilt motorhomes stand over 3m (10') high, so low bridges and tree branches can prove difficult both on the road and in campsites. The law requires that all vehicles 3m or over must display the vehicle height in the cab in both feet and metres. Coachbuilt motorhomes are referred to as low profile when the over-cab-bed is removed, thus reducing the overall vehicle height with the benefits of increased fuel economy and a better ride. Low-profile motorhomes are the most popular choice with retired French couples.

Villerest, France.

A-Class motorhomes look similar to a coach because the donor vehicle cab is not used. The smooth-lined body and purpose-built front end is built upon a bare chassis cowl (engine, electrics, axles, suspension, etc, but not the cab). The purpose-built front end has to be designed to be passenger and pedestrian-friendly (complying with European Community directive

Even in a car park we had a grand view from our A-Class Cityvan.

2007/46/EC), an expensive and time-consuming process. To make the most of the extra front end space the driver and co-pilot seats normally swivel around to become part of the lounge or dining area and a dropdown bed is often found above. Probably the best thing gained is the panoramic view out of the front windows.

Type Approval

Motorhome manufacturers had it quite easy concerning rules and regulations until European Community Whole Vehicle Type Approval (ECWVTA). This has been applicable for cars for many years and affected motorhomes from the 29th April 2009 when it was optional to undergo type approval for new models. From 29th April 2011 any new model launched had to undergo type approval and after 29th April 2012 all new motorhomes must conform to the ECWVTA supporting regulations. Type approval has removed many of the issues discussed below, but it is still a case of *caveat emptor*: Latin for buyer beware.

Weighty Issues

Prospective purchasers must understand the legal implications when buying a motorhome, especially concerning vehicle weights and driving licence restrictions. To be caught, or found to have been, driving a vehicle without the correct driving licence or to have overloaded your vehicle and thereby contributed to a fatal accident could well put you in a difficult position. Throughout this book we stress the importance of not overloading because of the effect this can have upon handling, safety and stopping distances – you have been warned!

When you pack a suitcase for air travel, you know there is a strict luggage allowance and this scenario is no different for motorhome travel. Payload is the automotive term used to describe the usable weight available for passengers, luggage, and goods. Chapter 4 explains the amount of payload your motorhome will need for you and your belongings.

Maximum Authorised Mass (MAM) may also be referred to as Maximum Vehicle Weight, Gross Vehicle Weight or Revenue Weight on vehicle documents. MAM is the legal maximum loaded weight of a vehicle, including all occupants. The MAM should be identified in the vehicle handbook and logbook. The definitive figures are shown on a plate or sticker fitted to the vehicle denoting weight specifications. The plate is

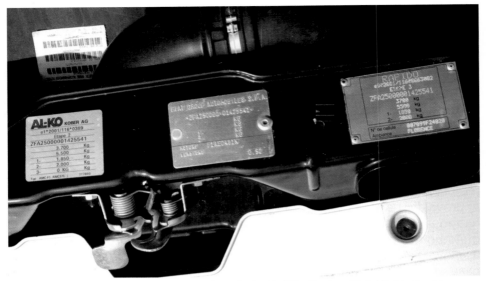

There may be more than one weight plate. Left: AL-KO, Centre: Fiat, Right: Rapido.

normally located in the engine housing and/or the footwells. Often there are two plates, the original from the chassis manufacturer and one from the converter. Converters can have the vehicle weight re-assigned both up and down, but usually only as high as the Maximum Technically Permissible Laden Mass (MTPLM) as specified by the chassis manufacturer, which includes overall weight and axle loadings.

Your driving licence may restrict you to driving vehicles with a MAM of 3,500kg or 7,500kg. For more information see driving licence restrictions on page 34. Motorhomes with a MAM over 3,500kg are often subject to speed restrictions across Europe, see page 214. Some countries charge higher road tolls and others, notably Austria, treat any vehicle over 3,500kg as commercial and expect them to comply with road rules applicable to commercial vehicles. Lowering the MAM of a motorhome to 7,500kg or 3,500kg is possible subject to leaving sufficient payload. The vehicle weight plate will be amended and the DVLA notified.

Motorhomes weighing more than 3,050kg unladen weight are restricted to 60mph instead of 70mph on UK dual carriageways and 50mph instead of 60mph on single-track national speed limit roads.

It would be reasonable to consider that motorhomes built upon a commercial vehicle chassis should have sufficient payload for normal use, enough to prevent illegal overloading. Unfortunately, this is not always the case and it is not as simple as looking at the payload figures printed in glossy brochures, especially on pre-type approved motorhomes. Manufacturers' calculations include, or exclude, different items in the unloaded weight, which is known as Mass In Running Order (MIRO) or Kerb Weight. MIRO refers to the entire manufactured weight of a vehicle including the equipment required for normal use. At the time of publication one manufacturer had written that their MIRO calculation accounted for the following: a 75kg (11st, 12lb) driver, engine coolants, and 90 per cent of the fuel, gas and water tank capacities.

Despite the EU calculation of MIRO, most people will 100 per cent fill the motorhome's fuel, fresh water and gas tanks. After all, you can't buy a 90 per cent full gas cylinder. For safety reasons, gas cylinders are filled to 80-87 per cent to allow for expansion. Does this mean that gas cylinder weight is calculated at 90 per cent of the 80-87 per cent? We have found examples where only one gas cylinder is included in the calculations, even though there is capacity for two, and aluminium cylinders are quoted instead of steel. Only 75kg is allocated for a driver into the MIRO, thus if the driver weighs 100kg, (15st, 9lb), the actual payload is reduced by 25kg. Motorhome manufacturers' weight plates may show the predetermined MIRO weight allocated to each model. Therefore, any optional extras fitted will increase the MIRO but will not be recorded on the vehicle weight plate. Increasingly no MIRO or payload is displayed on the weight plate.

	DETHLEFFS GmbH & Co.KG	
TYP I7870	e1*2001/116*0442*01	
	WDTI7870008386002	
	Blue text not original	Stufe 2
	MAM	5000 KG
08386002	*GTW*	6000 KG
	1– *Front axle*	2100 KG
	2– *First rear axle*	1500 KG
	3–*Second rear axle (tag)*	1500 KG

Dethleffs three axle motorhome weight sticker.

Go Motorhoming and Campervanning

Before European Community Whole Vehicle Type Approval (ECWVTA), the payloads displayed in different motorhome manufacturers' brochures and on vehicle weight plates were inconsistent. In an earlier edition of this book we published four pages of charts that showed data provided by manufacturers in 2005/6 in reference to MIRO and payloads for many motorhomes. Hymer included all 'essential habitation equipment' in their MIRO, allowing for a 75kg driver, 5kg electric cable, 68kg fuel (Ducato), 45kg gas cylinders, and water in tanks at 1kg per litre. In contrast, Geist and McLOUIS did not include anything, not even fuel. This equates to 293kg difference in the MIRO/payload weights for two similar motorhomes, assuming both have 100L water tanks and the same chassis type.

> **Shortlist cull**
> Choosing a motorhome is as easy as one, two, three.
> **1)** Draw up a shortlist.
> **2)** Remove all the motorhomes with less than 500kg payload.
> **3)** Buy one of the remainder.
> *If your list had no motorhomes with 500kg payload, read Chapter 4 before you buy.*

Buyers of pre-ECWVTA motorhomes are advised to ignore any payload figures provided and insist on seeing a weighbridge receipt with the total weight, axle weights and the relevant number plate printed on it. Assuming that no weighbridge receipt was available, we would insist on taking a prospective vehicle to a weighbridge. Stop negotiations if the seller is not willing to weigh the motorhome.

Each axle has a designated maximum weight limit and any vehicle driven on the public highway that is under the MAM but has an overloaded axle is contravening the law. The sum of the axle weights is more than the MAM as this allows for load variation. Axle weights are denoted on the vehicle weight plate and axles are always numbered from front to rear 1, 2, and 3

© Paul George

Wheelbase, overhang and user added weight.

when a tag axle is present. Motorhomes are at great risk of exceeding the rear axle loading, especially when built with a rear overhang exceeding 60 per cent. The most likely thing to cause an overloaded rear axle is 200-300kg of scooter and rack hanging on the back of a motorhome.

Public weighbridges are common in the UK and Europe. Visit www.chrishodgetrucks.co.uk to find one close to you. Weighing is normally chargeable but the operator may allow you to weigh for free without a printout. First, park with all wheels on the weigh plate and record the total weight. Next, weigh with only the front wheels on the weigh plate to get the front axle weight. You can also weigh the rear, however this weight is calculable by taking away the front axle weight from the total weight.

Gross Train Weight (GTW), referred to as Gross Combined Weight in the USA, is a higher figure than the MAM because GTW specifies the maximum combined weight of the vehicle plus a trailer. In theory it is possible to calculate the potential trailer weight by deducting the MIRO from the GTW. Because of the unique modifications made to most motorhomes, converters rarely recommend the maximum trailer weight denoted by the chassis manufacturer. Driving licence restrictions apply, see page 34.

Being caught driving a motorhome exceeding its MAM, GTW, or axle-loading will, at the very least, result in a verbal warning. Recovery companies clearly state they may not recover vehicles they deem to be overloaded and insurance companies may not pay out if they discover the vehicle you were travelling in was contravening the law. It may be possible to raise the payload of a motorhome by increasing the MAM. When buying

In the UK, weighbridges are normally manned. In Europe they can be self-service.

a new motorhome there may be an option to choose a higher MAM, check the technical specification section of sales brochures, but if you do choose to buy a motorhome with a higher MAM expect to wait three months whilst it is built. Increasing the MAM of a used motorhome is more complicated, and may not be possible at all. Often modifications to suspension, brakes, wheels, and tyres are necessary. Contact SvTech for professional advice, www.svtech.co.uk, Tel: 01772 621800.

Driving Licence Restrictions

If you passed your driving test in the UK before 1st January 1997, unless other restrictions apply, your licence will include category C1 with restriction 107 applied. This allows you to drive a vehicle with a MAM weight of 7,500kg and a GTW weight up to 8,250kg if towing a trailer. Drivers reaching the age of 70 will lose any entitlement to drive vehicles over 3,500kg unless a medical is passed and a Medical Examination Report is submitted to the DVLA.

If you passed your driving test after 1st January 1997, you have a category B licence and are entitled to drive a vehicle with a MAM of 3,500kg plus a 750kg trailer. Braked trailers over 750kg may be towed if the combined MAMs of the vehicle and trailer do not exceed 3,500kg, but the trailer MAM must be less than the tow vehicle unladen weight. If you wish to drive a vehicle heavier than 3,500kg you need to take a C1 driving test. Further information regarding driving licences and online forms are available from www.gov.uk/browse/driving, or pick up a form from the Post Office.

Australians, New Zealanders, Canadians, and Americans can drive a vehicle in Europe with a MAM up to 3,500kg for 12 months from date of entry. It is recommended that you buy an International Driver's Permit before you set off, see page 140.

The 2.1m (6'11") wide Cityvan can feel large in narrow lanes.

Size Matters

The maximum
permissible size of a
motorhome in the EU
is 12m (39'4") long
and 2.55m (8'4") wide.
A vehicle that has
passed an Individual
Vehicle Assessment
can have a maximum
width of 2.6m (8'6").
These measurements
exclude awnings,
mirrors, ladders,

*Pitch fees are sometimes proportionate to size.
Photo: Andy Glasgow.*

temporary bike racks, handholds, and the like. Most Coachbuilt and A-
Class motorhomes measure around 2.3m (7'7") wide. In reality a vehicle
2.3m wide often feels too wide on country lanes and in busy towns.
Campsites, road tolls, ferries, insurance, and recovery prices are often fixed
up to 6m. A 2.3m wide 6m long motorhome can be driven almost
everywhere and can sleep 4-5 people, but may feel very cramped on a
rainy day.

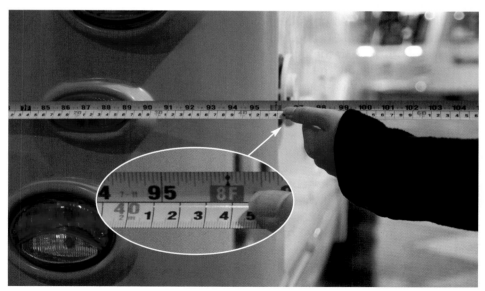

Some Bailey motorhomes are 2.44m (8') wide.

Six-metre rule – Six and below the benefits will show, six to seven is close to heaven but seven or more will be a chore.

Some motorhome manufacturers are prone to using the smallest chassis they can get away with. This keeps costs down, but sometimes creates an unnecessarily long rear overhang. Wheelbase is the distance between the centre points of the front and rear wheels. Rear overhang is the distance from the centre point of the rear wheel to the rear of the motorhome. Ideally, the overhang should be less than 55 per cent of the wheelbase to allow for towbars or bike racks, but we once measured a motorhome with a 71 per cent overhang. 60 per cent was the recognised limit and remains a good benchmark but has now been replaced by the following calculation. From a stationary position, when pulling away on a 12.5m-radius circle the rear of the vehicle must not swing out more than 0.8m. Large overhangs are easily scraped on uneven ground, steep ramps and they can sag, especially if overloaded. When parked alongside a wall, for example, do not turn the wheels to full lock and then drive away because you will probably tail-swipe the wall, as we once discovered.

Additional Considerations

Should you buy a left-hand-drive or right-hand-drive motorhome? There is no definitive answer, so consider whether you are going to drive mostly in the UK or Continental Europe. Visibility is impeded when you are driving the opposite hand-drive to the country, particularly at junctions and when overtaking. In addition, the caravan door will open roadside, not kerbside. We have owned five left-hand-drive and three right-hand-drive motorhomes. We prefer left-hand-drive motorhomes because most of our travel is Continental, but we have a right-hand-drive car for UK use. Left-hand-drive motorhomes generally have slightly lower second-hand values than their right-hand-drive counterparts.

One advantage gained from buying a new motorhome is that it will have a high-rated Euro engine, and therefore be accepted into most Low Emission Zone (LEZ) towns. LEZ towns are on the increase across the whole of Europe, so this is something to consider if you intend to drive into large towns and

Left or right, which side are you on?

Check your motorhome is winterised before heading to mountain resorts. Photo: Andy Glasgow at Passo d'Eira.

cities. Driving around LEZ towns is generally not a problem as the main routes are not included. If you want to visit a LEZ city, simply stop at an out-of-town site and use public transport to travel in. For more information, see www.urbanaccessregulations.eu.

Final manufacturing dates imposed by European emission standards. Light commercial vehicles (chassis) fitted with Euro-graded engines weighing more than 1,760kg up to 3,500kg.					
Euro 1	Euro 2	Euro 3	Euro 4	Euro 5	Euro 6
Oct 1994	Jan 1998	Jan 2001	Jan 2006	Sept 2010	Sept 2015
A "new motorhome" may actually be several years old because the chassis/engine could have been in storage for a long time before conversion and first registration may be years later. To confirm what Euro-graded engine is fitted contact the chassis manufacturer, quoting the chassis and engine numbers.					

Motorhomes do not have to pass any tests to prove they are suitable for use in cold conditions. The 1998 European standard EN1646 has three grades to define the heating ability of leisure vehicles with accommodation. The standard details how to test a vehicle, but there is no obligation to do so. A manufacturer can say the motorhome complies with EN1646 because the lowest grade, Grade 1, has no requirement to heat the motorhome or maintain a temperature difference between the inside and outside. Motorhomes do not have to undergo a cold environmental chamber test, but testing is the only way to prove that the stated grade is correct. The EN1646 Grade 2 and Grade 3 tests require the motorhome to be chilled in an environmental chamber so that the fabric of the motorhome and internal space are 0°C and -15°C respectively. The chamber temperature is maintained throughout the test at 0°C for Grade 2 and -15°C for Grade 3. Using the motorhome's onboard space heater, the internal temperature must reach 20°C within 45 minutes, and then maintain 20°C or more for two hours. Multiple points are monitored throughout the test. The standard requires that fresh water facilities work, but has no requirement for waste water.

Grade 2 is good enough for summer use, but Grade 3 is actually what is required for comfortable habitation. Motorhomes that have passed Grade 2 or 3 are not issued with a plate or sticker, but they may have supporting paperwork. To get definitive answers, contact the manufacturer and request a copy of the test results. The standard does not specify a level of insulation or heater

Is the waste water tank insulated and will it drain completely?

output. In theory, a motorhome could pass the test with poor insulation if it has a high output heater. Insulation is light, but the area covered is large so the weight becomes significant. Walls are a manufacturing compromise area because they need to be strong, light, thin, and thermally efficient. Thick walls do not guarantee good insulation.

Before heading to the mountains for winter sports, look in your seat lockers or between floor layers to confirm that the water tank is integral. Van Conversions often have under-slung fresh water tanks that are prone to freezing, though some have a layer of insulation. The only way to stop external tanks from freezing is by running a heating element. Double glazed windows in the living area of the motorhome are preferable; check the windows have internal screens or thick curtains to help reduce draughts.

Bailey Approach motorhome insulated water tank.

Example of Benimar roof, sidewall and floor construction.

Don't Buy Inside Out

If men are from Mars and women are from Venus, then alienation is possible. When it comes to motorhome buying, gender differences mean that you and your partner could be worlds apart. We have spent many hours at motorhome shows observing and questioning buyers, sellers, and owners. There is no doubt that the majority of motorhomes are purchased by heterosexual couples. We observed that women have a bigger influence in choosing a motorhome. We set about asking sales staff the following question, "Who chooses a motorhome, a man or a woman?" The snap answer was women, but we found that company stakeholders always gave considered responses and tended toward men. Sales staff agreed in general that women choose a motorhome based on the interior space, and that having agreeable furnishings and fabrics are key to a sale. With so many more important elements to consider, you must not be a soft touch for the furnishings.

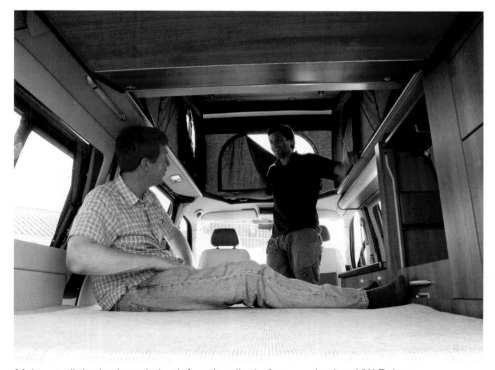

Make up all the beds and check functionality before purchasing. VW Reimo, www.conceptmulti-car.co.uk.

Men tend to look at motorhomes in a different way and are much more interested in functionality, construction, and drivability. We are sure that this is the right way to choose a motorhome and recommend that you agree the size and type of motorhome before you consider the interior. The motorhome should not be bigger than either partner is willing to drive. A bit more workspace here, a slightly bigger bathroom there, and a walk-around queen-size bed at the back soon add up.

The Living Accommodation

Compromise is the only word that explains the living situation and, despite countless layouts being designed, there is no easy way to squeeze a kitchen, bathroom, dining room, lounge, and bedrooms into a motorhome. There is no perfect motorhome layout and we have realised that it is best to buy for a specific task and not try to achieve a one-motorhome-fits-all option.

Our Peugeot Boxer Van Conversion was basic, but was great for taking stock to shows because it had a 1,000kg payload and a large load space under the rear dinette.

We imported this Hymer Camp 55 from Germany when the exchange rate was more favourable.

Over the past 15 years we have owned eight motorhomes and three caravans, each chosen for a task. We bought a 9m American LPG-driven RV to go Full-Timing, but found it unsuitable for the country lanes we like to drive. We quickly sold the RV and imported a 6.5m Hymer A-Class. Having returned from our tour of Europe we toured and worked in the UK, so we sold the Hymer and bought a Mazda Bongo day van and caravan. We got full-time jobs and bought a bigger caravan to live in whilst we were house hunting. We then bought a small Swift Coachbuilt, but sold it to fund the launch of Vicarious Books. We then imported another Hymer from Germany, but this time it was a 1993 Coachbuilt. We used it for Aire inspections, but found it too slow. Next we bought a DIY converted Peugeot Boxer van. We appreciated the extra speed and manoeuvrability, but during winter we felt like we were sleeping in a fridge. A PVC that is properly converted would not be cold and is completely suitable for our needs. In 2008 the Cityvan made by Pilote was the only non-PVC motorhome that suited our needs. Over the next four years we clocked up 59,500 miles in the Cityvan and slept in it for more than a years' worth of nights. We never really liked the internal layout and presumably nor did other people as very few were ever sold. In 2012 we replaced the Cityvan with the outgoing Pilote Aventura 600 TGA. The Aventura range replaced the Cityvan and remained the smallest A-Class motorhome in production. The Aventura range was widened in 2013 from 2.1m to 2.3m, presumably because Pilote believe that customers rate internal space over drivability.

Our Cityvan was purchased based on its external dimensions and payload.

Some people buy the wrong motorhome, or one that turns out to be too big for them because they think they need to accommodate occasional visiting friends or grandchildren. We suggest that you make guest accommodation a low priority when choosing your layout; after all, you can always put up a tent for them to sleep in.

This section will not tell you the ideal layout – only you can decide that – but it identifies elements that affect your enjoyment of a motorhome. Some designers give more attention to fashion and keeping costs down than functionality, but it's the little details that make a comfortable and practical motorhome.

Just big enough, is enough.

Bathroom – Some small motorhomes are built without a shower or toilet, which is fine if you always stop at campsites and don't mind trekking to the toilet block. A toilet is essential if you intend to Offsite-Park or use Motorhome Stopovers. However, a large bathroom is an unnecessary luxury as long as you can sit comfortably on the throne and have elbowroom in the shower. According to motorhome tester Dave Hurrell, 75cm is the minimum distance between the sink and anything behind you. People travelling with young children, or anyone less able bodied, may have to make a sacrifice somewhere else to have a large bathroom. Our preference is a wet room designed without a material shower curtain. This design is the most space efficient and is easily kept clean as every surface can simply be wiped down after showering. Prompt wiping down also reduces condensation.

Bedroom/Sleeping – Poor sleep can be a big problem. Roughing it for a week can be fun, but after a month you may not be laughing. The important factors are: access, space, construction, mattress quality, and condensation. Climbing up and down a ladder in the dark is definitely a skill, and clambering over your partner to get out of bed is less than romantic. A small bed soon becomes cramped

Combination fly screen and blackout blind.

after a day or two and a short bed will give you cold feet if they touch an outside wall. The dropdown bed in our A-Class Hymer was a fantastic use of space. It was easier to get into than over-cab beds and could be stowed away fully made up. However, the dropdown bed in our Cityvan had a serious design faux pas because it had to be extended before use and

Test the bed and also consider if there is sufficient height to increase mattress depth if required.

then it covered the hob, so a morning cup of tea could not be enjoyed in bed. Big rear lounge beds are great as they can be left made up and the rest of the motorhome functions as normal. Low beds are best in hot conditions. Over-cab beds can be cramped, difficult to get into and very hot, but rising heat is advantageous in winter. We are happy to use an over-cab bed, but we removed the dropdown bed from our Aventura because we did not need it. Significant weight was removed, which is particularly relevant considering we drive about 16,000 miles per year.

Four inches of foam is not sufficient to make a comfortable mattress and foam loses its spring with age. For the past two years we have been comfortably sleeping on a cheap memory foam mattress bought at Dunelm. We have previously had sprung mattresses made, but we will replace the memory foam mattress like-for-like if it loses its spring. Condensation can occur if there is insufficient ventilation under the mattress/cushions. If a table becomes part of a bed, the laminated surface will cause the cushions to become wet and mildew will attack the cushions if they are not properly aired. Bed slats prevent moisture building up and sprung slats improve comfort. Mattresses and special underlay liners that allow an air gap are available from www.shipshapebedding.co.uk. Seatbacks placed directly against cold outside walls also suffer condensation, but properly 'winterised' motorhomes will have air gaps behind seatbacks.

Check that the windows and vents are screened with both blackout blinds and mosquito-proof fly screens. The best design is a double roller system with the fly screen at the top and the blind at the bottom with the two clipped together. The blackout screen needs to be at the bottom so it can be dropped slightly in the morning to let in light but maintain modesty.

Kitchens only need to be just big enough.

Kitchen – Worktops are often cramped and cupboard space limited. Ensure there is enough space to prepare a meal, but, as with bathrooms, kitchens only need to be just big enough. Markets and supermarkets are much cheaper and have bigger ranges than campsite shops, so storing food and keeping it cool is a necessity. A fridge and a freezer, no matter how small, are essential, but we find bigger is better. The Thetford domestic-sized, under-worktop fridge-freezer fitted in our Aventura is just the right size and it maintains a very even temperature on all modes, but it does use a lot of gas. See page 63 to find out how fridges work. Check that a 230V socket is located so that you can safely boil a kettle. Three gas rings are adequate to cook most meals and a grill is an added bonus. Ovens are not standard in all European motorhomes, but are common in British makes and American RVs. However, ovens are far from essential and in every second-hand caravan/motorhome we have bought they appear to have been unused. Our personal view on ovens is that the loss of storage and additional weight and noise whilst travelling is not worth the occasional roast dinner. There are plenty of worktop electric ovens available and an electric oven is recommended for long-term campsite stays. BBQs and outdoor cookers reduce the need for an oven, but we found that we did not use our gas BBQ when we were Full-Timing, probably because we were constantly on the move and predominantly stopped at Motorhome Stopovers where BBQs are banned.

This Thetford under-worktop fridge is big enough.

Socialising And Lounging – On cold, wet days or mosquito-plagued evenings, you may be lounging or entertaining inside your motorhome for many hours. You will probably want to lounge with your feet up, especially when reading or watching TV, so consider where your back and feet will rest. The traditional dinette set-up can prove small and uncomfortable over

Dave Hurrell had a Van Conversion custom made with a good sofa opposite the sliding door to optimise the view.

long periods. L-shaped seating areas (still around a removable table) provide a more comfortable and sociable solution. As with mattresses, seat cushion foam deteriorates with age. Foam thickness is important, but sprung seat cushions prove more comfortable. Dual function design makes sense but is not always utilised. The driver and passenger chairs should swivel to become armchairs, known as captain's chairs, but these are often said to be too high when driving because of the swivel mechanism. The sofa and dining area should become beds without the use of the table, which should be free standing for indoor and outdoor use. Other design considerations include correct location of TV, lights, and sockets. Both our Swift and Cityvan had only one woefully inadequate and badly located 230V socket.

The socket in our Cityvan was badly located.

This Murvi motorhome has three belted passenger seats.

Belted seats – There are plenty of motorhomes with more berths than belted seats, but it is not practical to retrofit seatbelts so ensure your motorhome has enough belted seats for all your passengers. Because this scenario has not been tested in a court of law, in some circumstances, it is not illegal to carry adult passengers on unbelted rear seats in motorhomes. Realistically it is inadvisable to carry unbelted passengers.

Storage Space – Consider where you are going to store everything. Are there enough lockers and can you access them from both inside and outside? Does the wardrobe have sufficient space? Some motorhomes have garages (large lockers at the rear) designed for bicycles, motorbikes or micro cars. Some are converted to hold pets. Garages are not essential and are easy to overload, but they are

Caravanning inside out?

Dave Hurrell organised his storage to ensure there was space for everything he needed.

preferable for bike storage because bikes on outside racks get filthy in wet or dusty driving conditions no matter how well covered they are.

Disabled Motorhomers

Motorhome travel is well suited to people with mobility problems subject to the motorhome being adapted to suit individual requirements. The main advantages are a home-from-home experience with no reliance on third parties if you choose to stop at Motorhome Stopovers. Many campsites have disabled facilities and the most suitable campsite guide we know of is the ACSI DVD. This has a searchable database program that you can load onto a laptop. Each campsite's facilities are explained in detail including: toilets, showers, and access to other onsite amenities. There are 367 UK campsites 'suitable for the disabled' on the DVD and 4,002 across the Continent. ACSI inspect all 8,539 sites listed on the DVD every year. You can purchase a copy from www.Vicarious-Shop.com, Tel: 0131 208 3333.

Several converters carry out alterations to new and second-hand vehicles. Nirvana Motorhomes has a "try-before-you-buy" scheme for disabled motorhomers and they offer Van Conversions and fully accessible Coachbuilt motorhomes, visit www.simplywav.co.uk, Tel: 0800 3281475. Coachbuilt GB specialise in adapting motorhomes, caravans and holiday homes, visit www.coachbuiltgb.co.uk, Tel: 02476 341196. Motorhomes bought

WildAx can convert PVCs for your needs, including hoists, visit www.wildaxmotorhomes.com, Tel: 01422 372111.

Motorhome adapted and photographed by Coachbuilt GB.

for use by a disabled person may not be subject to VAT. See VAT Notice 701/7, http://customs.hmrc.gov.uk, Tel: 0845 010 9000.

MMM magazine includes a mobility supplement every November; back issues available, Tel: 01778 392496. Also see Queen Elizabeth's Foundation for Disabled People, www.qef.org.uk, Tel: 01372 841100, the Forum of Mobility Centres, www.mobility-centres.org.uk, Tel: 0800 5593636, and www.wheelgotravelling.info which is a personal site with useful information.

The Price Is Right

Consider both the purchase price and running costs of your motorhome. Factor in insurance, servicing and recovery charges as well as fuel economy. Prices range from £1,000 to over £1,000,000, so it is easy to get carried away. You will probably find that you need to spend more than you originally thought. With some negotiation, £32,000 will buy you a brand new entry-level motorhome. £10,000 will buy a good 20-year-old motorhome. Under £10,000, there are plenty of Van Conversions, VW Campervans and Coachbuilt motorhomes aged 15-30 years.

Motorhomes: the most expensive plug in appliance?

Motorhomes have an average life of 25 years and do not depreciate as quickly as cars. Mid-life motorhomes hardly depreciate year to year. In 2003 brand new budget Coachbuilt motorhomes started at £20,000, but their equivalents now start at £35,000. Second-hand budget 2003 motorhomes are now worth between £12,000 and £20,000.

Motorhomes for sale at The National Motorhome show Peterborough.

Most UK-owned motorhomes are very low mileage. Gentleman Jack's 2014 research for Practical Motorhome found that UK-owned Coachbuilt motorhomes average 3,700 miles per year. Europeans tend to clock up high mileage in their motorhomes, mostly because they will happily spend a few hours on the motorways to pop into another country for the weekend. High mileage motorhomes can be perfectly serviceable and can be purchased considerably cheaper.

When buying second-hand, age and mileage are no more important than wear and tear. Check the overall condition including the chassis/underneath, engine, and running gear. Check the seals and trims on the outside for cracks, sun damage, or knocks and scrapes. Inside check carpets, cupboards, handles and upholstery. Be aware of any

When buying second-hand check for wear and tear.

Personalisation can devalue a motorhome. Painted murals are like motorhome tattoos.

personalisation and DIY as this often reduces the value. Water ingress is a problem and must be checked for, but can normally be cured. Long-term damp has a distinctive smell, mildew in cupboards is a sign, but an inexpensive damp meter is worth taking along to viewings. Water penetration can cause floors to delaminate, a bouncy feeling is a telltale sign, but delamination is repairable. Ensure, by testing, that all gas/electricity parts are working. An older motorhome in excellent condition may be preferable to a younger one in poor condition.

Gadgets and gizmos above the basic motorhome specification can be nice to have, but may not add any value. Draw up a 'must-have' list and try not to be swayed by extras which are not on it. Remember, extras can add considerable weight and, apart from proper alarms, solar panels, and awnings, are relatively cheap to add later. See Chapter 4 – Preparing Your Motorhome.

Design and function are not necessarily the same thing.

A handful of manufacturers produce the domestic appliances fitted in most European-built caravans and motorhomes, therefore any caravan/motorhome retailer should be able to service and supply parts. Parts and repairs on European base vehicles are also not a problem. American and Japanese parts, however, can be expensive and difficult to source.

You can look at the MOT history of any vehicle three years old or older at www.MOTinfo.gov.uk, Tel: 0906 1209941, details are provided on the back of MOT certificates. You will need the vehicle registration number and either the document reference number from the V5C registration certificate or the MOT test number from the current MOT certificate. The database goes back to 2005 making it possible to track mileage and see failure and advisory notices. Motorhomes should have annual engine and chassis service, a habitation inspection, and a damp check. Most motorhome owners keep the supporting paperwork, but once a motorhome has changed hands a few times this paper trail frequently goes missing.

Where To Buy

You can do a lot of armchair research on the internet. Visit www.motorhomemarket.co.uk, www.ebay.co.uk, www.gumtree.com, www.autotrader.co.uk or type in 'motorhome classified ads' into your web browser. For European motorhome prices visit www.mobile.de, the German equivalent of Auto Trader, and www.lemondeducampingcar.fr, a French camping car magazine publisher. The 'free ads' papers are a good source of cheaper motorhomes.

Dealers offer choice, but they may only stock motorhomes from one manufacturer.

Visiting local motorhome dealers is a good starting point because you will be able to see many different motorhomes, although often only from one manufacturer's range. Buying a second-hand motorhome from a dealer affords a greater level of consumer

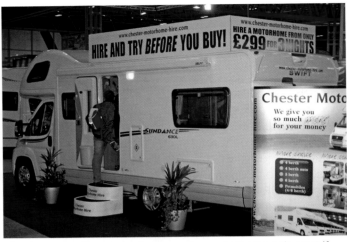

Hire fees are often deducted from the motorhome sale cost if purchased after hiring.

protection than from a private seller. You are likely to pay more from a dealer, but you should also get a warranty.

Benchmark Motorhomes
The following campervans and motorhomes have been in production for many years making it possible to use them in comparison whether you are looking to buy new or second-hand.
VW Conversions: VW California. Bilbo's Design, Celeste T4 and Celex T5.
Large Panel Van Conversions: Murvi Morello. Auto-Sleeper Symbol. Adria Twin.
Coachbuilt Motorhomes: Elddis Autoquest range. Chasson Flash range.
A-Class: Hymer B544.

Outdoor motorhome shows attract dealers and manufacturers from all over the country. They will be showing the majority of brands, both new and second-hand, but there are no second-hand motorhomes at the indoor NEC shows. The September shows may have dealers selling off the current year's stock in preparation for new models. Shows are held all over the country and are advertised in all the magazines and listed on www.worldofmotorhomes.com. Ticket offers are normally available through the camping/caravan clubs as well as motorhome clubs. If you are going to your first show and it is one of the bigger ones, give yourself two days. On day one look at every type of motorhome from RVs to micro campers, on day two only look at the size and type of motorhome that you have decided upon. Dealers should have a wealth of information, so ask plenty of questions. Try to imagine how you will live in the motorhome. Sit in the living space, pretend to cook a meal or have a shower, and make the bed up. Thousands of motorhomes are sold at shows, with no test drives! If it is second-hand, there will be no weighbridge certificate or possibility of taking a prospective motorhome to a weighbridge.

There is no reason why you should not buy a long way from home and you may have to for some European makes and for second-hand motorhomes if you want a specific model. Many dealers have overnight facilities to use whilst motorhomes are in for servicing. If you have niggling problems, these will be more of an issue if your dealer is far away. If you decide to buy new, use the listings in the back of motorhome magazines to get the phone numbers of all the relevant dealers and see what you can negotiate over the phone.

Private sales are often priced much higher than they actually sell for. Response to adverts can be low, so you should be able to negotiate. Comprehensive motorhome warranties are available from the AA, see www.aawarranty.co.uk.

Also read Selling Your Motorhome, on page 61, as it discusses the tricks and essentials for a quick and profitable sale.

Importing From Europe

Importing a motorhome from Europe is relatively easy, but the viability fluctuates with the euro exchange rate. When the rate is favourable considerable money can be saved. Comparatively few European motorhome brands are sold in the UK compared to those that are available from Germany, France, and Italy. Germany has the biggest motorhome market, so is the most likely place to import one from. The only problem with buying an unknown brand or model is that it may prove harder to sell back in the UK.

Camper export document, German DVLA equivalent.

Before you import a vehicle from the EU, contact the DVLA to check for any changes in forms or procedures, www.gov.uk/importing-vehicles-into-the-uk, Tel: 0300 7906802.

First, you must notify HMRC that you have brought a vehicle into the UK using the Notification of Vehicle Arrivals (NOVA) system. This must be done within 14 days of the vehicle arriving in the UK to avoid a late notification penalty charged at £5 per day. NOVA replaces VAT Form 414, 415 and C&E 386 which were previously used to calculate tax on imported vehicles. Once your NOVA application is processed, you will be informed how much VAT is due. Foreign dealers will charge local VAT and you will also have to pay UK VAT when you import the vehicle. However, once you have the UK Certificate of VAT you can post it to the seller for a local VAT refund. Ensure you discuss this in advance of purchase.

All vehicles imported from the EU will require a European Certificate of Conformity; however, left-hand-drive vehicles manufactured after 29th April 2012 will also require a certificate of Mutual Recognition from the Vehicle Certification Agency (fees apply). In order to be awarded this certificate, your vehicle must be suitable to drive in Britain and you must be able to prove that you have made any necessary alterations to achieve this (i.e. headlights dip to the left, fog light on the offside, and the speedometer displaying miles per hour graduations that are visible at night).

Next, you will need to register your vehicle with the DVLA. You will need to request either form V55/5 (used vehicles) or V55/4 (new vehicles) and an import pack. Vehicles over three years old will need to pass an MOT. For new vehicles you will also need form V267. A vehicle is classed as new only if it has not been sold by a retailer before, is less than six months old, has less than 6,000km recorded, has not been previously permanently registered, and is a current model or has ceased production within the last two years. Older vehicles that have not been previously registered will be considered second-hand.

The following documents (originals, not photocopies) need to be sent or taken to your local DVLA office when you register the vehicle:

- Form V55/5, if used, or V55/4, if new
- MOT certificate, if the vehicle is more than three years old
- £55 registration fee, if new
- V267, if new
- Vehicle insurance certificate
- Any documents you have relating to the vehicle and all export papers including the equivalents of the UK V5C Registration Certificate which shows the date of first registration (see photo on opposite page)
- Personal identification: photo or paper driving license, passport, birth/marriage certificate
- Confirmation of address: recent utility bill, bank statement, council tax bill

All imported vehicles need to be stored off the public highway until registration is completed. UK residents are not allowed to use non-UK registered vehicles on UK roads. Fully comprehensive insurance is not available during the importation of vehicles across mainland Europe. Some companies offer insurance against the chassis number once it reaches the UK. Currently the only satisfactory solution is to have the vehicle delivered.

If this all sounds like too much effort or risk, Bundesvan will assist you through the whole process, see www.bundesvan.co.uk or call Nick on 01803 606335. The key advantages offered are no insurance risk on the drive back to the UK, no foreign money transfer, and no double VAT on new vehicles.

German temporary exportation number plates.

John Kelly's self-build. SBMCC member.

Build It Yourself

Self-building a motorhome can save you money and allow you to create a bespoke vehicle for your desires or needs. The first time you use it will give you a real sense of achievement, but the reality is that building a motorhome will be difficult and extremely time consuming and should only be taken on by people with a history of completing projects. Three months is the minimum build time and £5,500 will fund a budget conversion. Purchasing an accident-damaged caravan is a good way to acquire many of the parts that you will need.

Most people convert a panel van because this is the simplest option. To reregister the vehicle as a Motor Caravan with the DVLA it must pass a 'reasonableness test' to prove that it is a 'motor caravan' which is defined as:

A special purpose M1 category vehicle which…is constructed to include living accommodation which contains at least the following equipment.
- *seats and table,*
- *sleeping accommodation which may be converted from the seats,*
- *cooking facilities, and*
- *storage facilities.*
This equipment shall be rigidly fixed to the living compartment.

The classification goes on to say, "the table mounting arrangement must be secured as a permanent feature…although the table may be detachable." You can read the entire definition of a motor caravan in the Individual Vehicle Approval (IVA) Manual for vehicle category M1 available from DVSA.

Self-build kits can reduce workload, leaving you to do the bits you are interested in. Alternatively, commission a company to build your motorhome. Ensure you specify in writing what you require in as much detail as possible. Specify exact products to be used and detail the finishes that you would like. This is the only way to prevent a difficult situation if the finished motorhome does not live up to your expectations. Keep in mind that self-build motorhomes will not achieve the same resale price as a recognised brand.

John Kelly, member of the Self Build Motor Caravanners' Club, www.sbmcc.co.uk, detailed his motorhome self-build costs 2009/10.

Item	Cost	Item	Cost
8 year old, high mileage, extra long wheelbase Iveco Daily 35 s11	£2,600	12v cable (new)	£32
		Replacement cab roof lining (new)	£72
Crash damaged, 4 year old Avondale Osprey caravan	£2,000	Fresh water tank (new)	£40
		Grey waste tank (used)	£20
Collecting caravan	£70	Bicycle rack (salvaged used)	£0
Timber and ply (new)	£360	Bicycle rack repair and fittings	£37
Replacement driver and passenger seats (used)	£42	Water inlet and pipe (new)	£22
		Mains hook up inlet (new)	£14
Passenger seat swivel base (used)	£25	Sealants and glues (new)	£67
Seat adapter plates (new)	£20	Screws and fixings (new)	£64
Sink and drainer (new)	£100	TV/DVD (new)	£110
Leisure battery (new)	£65	TV aerial (new)	£60
Truma 'warm air' heater (used)	£150	Aerial mounting pole (new)	£13
Shower tray (new)	£25	Awning light (new)	£25
Shower and W/C wall cladding panels (new)	£110	Spare wheel cover (new)	£18
		Van graphics	£50
Shower curtain (new)	£8	Carbon monoxide alarm (new)	£28
Shower mat	£10	Smoke alarm (new)	£6
Mini Heki rooflights (new)	£160	Fire blanket (new)	£15
3 LED ceiling lights (new)	£40	Fire extinguisher	£12
Small fluorescent strip light (new)	£15	Cupboard & under seat storage bins	£32
Rockwool wall insulation	£20	Angle iron for water tank brackets	£18
Carpet for wall and ceiling covering (new)	£80	12v light switches	£18
		Cab floor carpet	£20
Floor insulation boards (new)	£18	Pressure activated water pump	£68
Floor vinyl (new)	£40	Inverter	£38
Fiamma awning fixing kit	£48	Step edging plate	£14
Fiamma wind out awning (used)	£180	Table leg and table mounting bar	£20
Damaged caravan awning (to make 'safari' room)	£50	2 x 10 litre drinking water containers	£16
		Silver screens	£60
Kitchen worktop (new)	£35	**Conversion cost**	**£7,385**
Replacement toilet cassette (new)	£60	Overhaul van brakes	£250
Gas fittings (new)	£20	Sales of surplus caravan parts, windows and heater	-£150
Cooker repair	£25		

Anyone considering building their own motorhome should read *Build Your Own Motorhome* by John Wickersham, available from www.Vicarious-Shop.com, and visit the Self Build Motor Caravanners' Club website, www.sbmcc.co.uk. Other useful websites include: www.rainbowconversions.co.uk, www.deepredmotorhome.com, www.charlesandson.co.uk, and www.magnummotorhomes.co.uk.

The Buyer's Checklist

Few sellers will give you an in-depth description about their motorhome unless you ask the right questions. You can save yourself wasted journeys by asking the following questions, preferably over the phone. The first question is a good warm up before the interrogation begins.

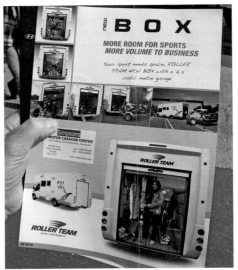

The payload of the 3,500kg Roller Team Box is 510kg, with the rear garage limited to 400kg.

- Please describe the layout of the motorhome starting from the cab. Are the cab seats captain's chairs and do they swivel? Is there a separate bathroom with toilet and shower? Where are the beds and what size are they? Is the floor carpeted and is it removable?
- What is the overall size of the motorhome?
- How long have you owned it and why are you selling?
- How often and where did you use the motorhome? How many miles has it done, how many have you done in it, and how many in the last year?
- Is it diesel or petrol? What capacity is the engine, is it powerful enough uphill and on the motorway? How many miles to the gallon? Does it use any oil?
- Is there any damage to the vehicle? Has it been accident repaired? Is there sun damage?
- What repairs have been done? Has it had a new exhaust? How old are the tyres?
- What is the MAM and payload? Does the MIRO weight include full fuel tank, driver, full water tank, and full gas cylinders? If the seller is unsure or blasé then the likelihood is they may have been using it overloaded.
- What service history does it have? Does it have its original documents (manuals)? When did it have its last MOT, engine chassis and habitation service and by whom?
- So that you can look at the MOT history ask for the vehicle registration number and either the document reference number from V5C registration certificate or the MOT test number from the current MOT certificate.
- Is anything not working properly or broken?
- Is there, or has there ever been, any damp?

- What is the interior condition like? Where are the marks, scuffs, or wear? How worn are the cushion covers? Is the foam starting to show signs of age? How clean/worn are the carpets?
- Has it had any DIY alterations or paint jobs?
- What kind of heating system does it have?
- What hot water system is there? Does it run on gas, electricity, or both?
- How large is the water tank? Where is it located and is any filter system fitted?
- How does the toilet system work and how much capacity do the toilet and waste water tanks have?
- Is the fridge compressor or 3-way? Does it have a freezer compartment?
- Are there blinds and fly-screens on the windows and top vents?
- Is there enough storage space? Are there any externally accessible lockers?
- What capacity is the leisure battery in amp hours? How old and how easy is it to access? Are there any 12V sockets? Does the motorhome have electric hook-up? Is the cable included? Where are the internal plug sockets located and how many are there?
- What security features does it have, i.e. locks and alarms?
- What add-ons or extras come with it?
- How many and what size gas cylinders does it take? Are the gas cylinders included?
- Can you arrange for us to take the motorhome to a weighbridge during our test drive?
- What warranty is included and what are the conditions, i.e. return to base or Europe-wide?
- How did you come to the advertised price and have you since reduced it? Only ask this question toward the end as it may affect the way a seller answers further questions.

Left: Check the bed construction and storage space.
Right: Check the ground clearance. Steps and pipes can catch on uneven ground.

We have found that a private seller who answers these questions confidently and willingly is probably selling a motorhome in the condition described. The main problem will be convincing them that they should sell you the motorhome at the price you think it's worth. When the alleged owner answers questions poorly, is evasive or repeatedly says, "It's a good runner – a really nice camper", then the chances are you will see a different motorhome to the one you had in mind. Expect to be on the phone for at least 20 minutes and, unless you are completely sure, don't bother driving a long distance to see a private sale motorhome. Equally, don't fall in love with it before you've seen it. One final point, people prefer you to be honest, so whether on the phone or at a viewing, if it is not right for you stop there and tell them so and why. A departing, "I will think about it" when you have no intention of buying it is very frustrating for the seller.

Test drives are essential. Insurance is likely to be a problem because it is unlikely that either your own car or the seller's motorhome insurance will allow you to drive with comprehensive cover. You can learn a lot from the passenger's seat. Look for clutch travel and whether the driver uses the pedal as a footrest. Listen and watch for smooth gear changes, including reverse. Take the vehicle on a dual carriageway, up a steep hill, and on twisty roads, all of these will give an overall impression of running condition. In addition, reverse up a steep hill to ensure there is no clutch judder. Take the opportunity to visit a weighbridge and find out exactly what payload is available.

Motorhomes for sale at The National Motorhome Show, Peterborough.

Seriously consider having any prospective motorhome professionally inspected. Motoring recovery organisations and several national companies will carry out base vehicle visual inspections, but they will not be able to comment on the 'caravan' elements. The best option, if possible, would be to take it to a motorhome service centre.

2001 Nissan 2.2 diesel 5speed manual, midi size coachbuilt, new Nu Venture body in build now, toilet compartments with cassette toilet
£18,500

Selling Your Motorhome

The starting point of any second-hand sale is working out how much the motorhome is worth. Depreciation is inevitable, but how much depends on age and condition. Do not overprice your motorhome because it will probably waste both time and money. Private sale motorhomes, no matter what value, sell for £2,000-£3,000 less than comparable motorhomes advertised on dealer forecourts. The Warners' magazines – *MMM*, *Which Motorhome/Caravan* and *Motorhome Mart* – run the same classified adverts. These are also displayed online at www.outandaboutlive.co.uk. According to Carly from Warners, most motorhomes are sold within three months, but each time the advert is renewed the sale price is reduced by £1,000. Motorhomes priced on the cheap side of realistic sell very quickly, often from the website before the magazines are printed. Motorhome dealers will often negotiate a price over the phone, but they will err on the side of caution. Local dealers will probably want to see your motorhome, either at their premises or yours. This gives them the opportunity to assess a fair price, but also to charm you. Once you have a trade price you can compare it with private and dealer adverts for similar motorhomes. Remember, the dealers mark up between £1,000 to 50 per cent of the value. *MMM* publishes a six-part second-hand price guide, but this only shows dealer forecourt prices of available models. Part-exchanging is unlikely to be the most economical, but offers a simple solution. Additional equipment does not necessarily add value, but it may make your motorhome more sellable. Remember that any DIY, repairs or personalised interior/exterior design will probably lower the value if it does not appear to be a professional job.

Clean the motorhome thoroughly inside and out (dealers do) and remove anything that is not included in the sale. Provide as much information about the vehicle as possible, and have it MOT tested. If you are selling from your drive, make the area presentable and park so the motorhome can be inspected on all sides. Finally, don't warm up the engine before a viewing because it will make buyers suspicious about its starting ability. Batteries are affordable, so replace them if necessary.

Clean your motorhome roof before you sell it.

Most prospective buyers have an idea of what they want, but may not know much about your specific model. Use the Buyer's Checklist on page 58 and try to answer the questions whether they are asked or not. It is worth asking over the phone what models they like and how they intend to use the motorhome. We always follow this process because it is not worth wasting everybody's time viewing an unsuitable motorhome. Where should you advertise? We have had good responses from the free classifieds websites, so try these first. We have also had some success with Auto Trader. When selling, the endless sales calls from people wanting to send free information or having buyers looking for a "Winnebago campervan" are frustrating. Don't be discouraged by callers who arrange to view only to cancel on the day. Remember, you also had no idea what you wanted at some stage.

Meaningful test drives are essential.

Test drives may be expected, but it is unlikely that a prospective buyer has sufficient insurance cover. If they say they have, ask for proof. If you, as a seller, have fully comprehensive 'any driver' insurance, check the small print for age or penalty restrictions. Personally, if a buyer with relevant insurance really wants to drive we would take them to a deserted car park. Beware people do steal vehicles whilst on test drives or viewings, so stay with them at all times whilst they have access to the keys.

Further Information

Auto Trader has detailed information with tips for buyers and sellers at the start of its magazines and online at www.autotrader.co.uk. This information details everything from how to write your advert to what questions to ask and the importance of security checking the vehicle for damage, theft, or outstanding finance.

CHAPTER 3 – Life Support: An Idiot's Guide

Motorhomes have everything required for a day or more away from civilisation; and the more you know about how things work, the better your trips will be. This chapter could be considered an induction for motorhome occupants, and is written in the KISS style: Keep It Simple, Stupid. Some subjects are so important that they are explained in depth so that you can make the most of your motorhome. To bring things into perspective, real life examples have been provided. Onboard utilities include electricity, gas, and water, and these can last up to seven days with frugal use.

Switched On

Although water is fundamental to life, water will not flow from motorhome taps unless there is a source of electricity. Most motorhomes have three interlinked electrical systems controlled by a panel located in the living area. The base vehicle has a 12V engine starter battery that powers all the driving related electrical items. The habitation area has its own wiring system and 12V battery known as a leisure battery. This is essential to prevent the engine battery from discharging (going flat). The habitation area also has a 230V mains circuit that is usable when a mains supply is available.

To understand how the three electrical systems are interlinked we will look at how a 3-way absorption refrigerator operates. Most motorhomes have a 3-way absorption refrigerator, whereas your fridge and freezer at home use compressors to propel the refrigerant liquid around the metal tubes; you have probably heard the motor/compressor running. Few motorhomes are

This Truma control provides simple, accurate 12V and water levels. In addition, there are gas and electric heater controls.

fitted with compressor fridges because of the noise, but also they can consume a considerable amount of 12V electricity. A 3-way absorption fridge requires a heat source to drive the cooling process. Heat causes the refrigerant to expand and the pressure pushes the refrigerant around the system, this is known as a heat pump. Three energy sources provide the heat: either a 12V or 230V electrical element or by burning gas. Old motorhomes may have fridges that can run on gas without any electrical supply, but typically there will be a control panel managing the fridge and this will draw small amounts of power from the leisure battery.

Van converters sometimes install small 12/24V compressor fridges to save space. Compressor fridges do not burn gas, thus a smaller gas locker/bottle can be used. However, when an under-worktop size compressor fridge is running with no alternative power supply, it will flatten an 110Ah leisure battery within one and a half days. Additional leisure batteries can be installed, but bear in mind they weigh between 25kg-30kg each. Compressor fridges do suit expedition vehicles which are driven all day because the fridge is powered by the alternator and in addition they perform better than absorption fridges in high temperatures. That said, the standard 3-way absorption fridges fitted in our motorhomes have worked fine on gas in temperatures up to 37°C. If your fridge does not perform well in hot climates, and you have confirmed that it is correctly installed, a low consumption 12V computer fan can be used to increase airflow through the top vent.

The Banner leisure battery, on the left, has been designed for repeated deep discharging.

Most onboard facilities require 12V to operate, including the water pump, lights, and the heating system. Available power is determined by the batteries' capacity, condition, and charge state.

Motorhomes normally have lead-acid batteries (wet batteries) for both engine starting and leisure use. Gel batteries are more expensive than wet batteries and are normally used in boats because they do not produce gas during charging and are spill proof. Absorbed Glass Mat (AGM) batteries are built for extreme use applications such as powering forklifts and golf carts.

Starter battery construction enables high energy, rapid discharge, and quick recharge. Repeated slow or over discharge is likely to degrade the thin lead plates. Leisure batteries have thicker lead plates and extra reinforcement to enable frequent deep discharge without damage. When you buy a leisure battery make sure it is labelled in accordance with directive EN50342. See the photos for correctly labelled leisure batteries.

Leisure battery capacity is rated in ampere-hours (Ah). This would suggest that a 100Ah battery should be capable of delivering 1A for 100 hours. Batteries give up more power when discharged slowly and less when rapidly discharged, this is known as Peukert's law. Correctly labelled batteries display the 20-hour nominal capacity. The capacity is determined by three controlled discharge tests at three different amp loadings. The battery voltage is monitored and the test stops when the voltage drops to 10.5V.

This Banner leisure battery displays three amp hour ratings.

This Varta leisure battery displays two amp hour ratings.

Go Motorhoming and Campervanning

You can only know what size leisure battery you need by calculating the number of Ah you think you will use between charges. To do this, work out the amperage of all the items you will use (or would like to use) and for how long. Amps can be calculated by dividing power (watts) by voltage, for example, a 1,000W/230V fan heater runs at 4.35A, 1,000W / 230V = 4.35A. If the fan heater could run on 12V it would use 83.33A per hour! Clearly a problem if only one 75Ah battery is available. Furthermore, the higher the load, the fewer Ah are available as can be seen by the three figures quoted on the battery label. You can find an online calculator at www.bannerbatterien.com. In reality, most motorhomes are fitted with one 75-110Ah leisure battery, so if you divide the figure you had previously calculated by 10 you may be closer to the reality. A second battery can be run in parallel, but it must be properly installed, fused, secured, and vented. The basic rules are that the batteries need to be the same age, type, and capacity. They are connected together positive-to-positive, negative-to-negative. This type of connection makes the two batteries behave as one, but the charger will stop once one of the batteries is fully charged. Therefore, it is no good connecting a 75Ah to a 100Ah battery because the 100Ah battery will never fully charge. When two equal capacity batteries are run in parallel, both should reach full charge unless one develops a fault which reduces its capacity.

According to manufacturers, the optimum operating temperature for a battery is around 27°C (80°F). Available battery power reduces approximately one per cent per 1°C fall in temperature. Therefore, at freezing point a battery's capacity reduces by approximately 27 per cent.

Two 100Ah leisure batteries connected in parallel.

Standard 110Ah lead-acid leisure batteries are suitable for most motorhome and caravan users. They are far cheaper than AGM or gel alternatives and, if they are looked after, will perform well for several years. Keep lead acid batteries topped up with demineralised water and charge occasionally during lay-up periods as a battery can lose up to 1 per cent charge per day even without taking into account drain from clocks or alarms. People who will always hook-up to the mains, or will only stop a night or two away from mains hook-up, need only buy a 75Ah capacity leisure battery.

Lead-acid batteries do not physically store electricity. Electricity is actually created on demand by chemical reaction; in brief, ions and electrodes transfer between the lead plates. This process is reversed during charging. To keep a lead-acid battery in top condition it is necessary to apply 14.4V or more during charging. Charging at 14.4V or slightly more has a rejuvenating effect, but as a by-product hydrogen gas and oxygen are produced and need to be vented outside for safety. To replace the lost hydrogen and oxygen, demineralised water (H_2O) should be periodically added to the battery cells.

Mains-powered battery chargers are normally specific to battery type because most gel batteries must not be charged over 14.4V to prevent gassing. Battery chargers can have sophisticated charging regimes and the better the charger, the better the charge. In reality, new motorhomes are likely to have adequate chargers fitted. A cheap starter battery charger is unlikely to perform as desired when used to charge a leisure battery. The charge rate in amps should be 10 to a maximum of 20 per cent of the battery's Ah capacity (i.e. 7.5A-15A per hour for a 75Ah battery and 10A-20A per hour for a 100Ah battery).

Battery to battery chargers are sophisticated intermediaries that work when the engine is running. Initially, they boost the normal 14V produced by the alternator so that the leisure battery can not only be fully charged, but can also charge in a shorter time. Several lower voltage charging regimes are applied during the process to achieve full charge. This type of charger would be a valuable asset to people that rarely use mains hook-up and stop for long periods with short driving times between stops. For further information visit www.conrad-anderson.co.uk, Tel: 0800 2790085 and www.roadpro.co.uk, Tel: 01327 312233.

Inverter powering a netbook.

Go Motorhoming and Campervanning

Inverters convert 12V DC (direct current) battery power into 230V AC (alternating current) mains equivalent voltage. Inverters are most efficient at maximum capacity and efficiency drops quickly as the load reduces, so do not buy one with more capacity than you need. We recommend you write a list of the items that you wish to power and speak to a specialist before choosing appliances or an inverter. Many motorhomers use inverters to run their satellite systems or laptops, but there are many 12V appliances available ranging from kettles and hairdryers, to televisions and microwave ovens, so consider these before opting for an inverter. Using appliances with a higher capacity than the 12V DC system can cope with may result in a blown fuse or cables and sockets overheating, which in turn could damage the appliance or start a fire. We recommend a short dedicated connection between the leisure battery and the inverter. Sterling Power Products Ltd specialises in inverters, visit www.sterling-power.com, Tel: 01905 771771.

12 Volt Electricity Consumption – The Reality

One 75Ah battery powering only the water pump and lights, when necessary, will have sufficient power for a pitched week during the summer. We monitored 298 continuous days away, during which we hooked up for 86 nights. We would have hooked up for only 11 nights had electricity not been included in campsite fees. We are not alone in this usage as most tourers we meet follow the same practices. The longest we have solely relied on one 110Ah battery between charges is two summer weeks, without TV. People who are touring and driving every few days should find they charge their motorhome batteries sufficiently without the need of electric hook-up.

Electric Hook-Up

Most UK campsites provide 16A electric hook-up, whereas hook-up at campsites in mainland Europe can be as low as 3A. Some campsites offer a choice of hook-up, rated at 6A, 10A, or higher, and you are charged accordingly. When paying for mains electricity, it is worth getting value for money, but

Two 16A circuit breakers, one RCD.

there is no point carrying high-power appliances that could trip the supply. Items that are worth their weight are: a low watt kettle, a cooking ring, and a dual function fan heater/cooling fan; everything else is a luxury you could take if you have weight and space available.

Any electrical appliance that has a heating element is likely to be rated at 1,000W or more. As previously discussed, a 1,000W device runs at 4.35A (1,000W/230V=4.35A), which means it cannot be used when hooked up to a 3A current. A 3A supply should allow you to run the motorhome fridge, thus saving gas, as well as low watt devices like a laptop computer. Charged leisure batteries are maintained using a low current charge, but the battery charger may trip the electrical supply if the batteries are flat and require a high input charge. Onboard water heaters that have a mains element draw about 2.75A.

Thermostatic portable heaters often have step heat/power levels. The picture of the heater control knob with the three power consumption settings shows the Glasgows' foolproof way of preventing circuit breakers from tripping. You can easily see what capacity supply is available by looking at the circuit breakers. The picture above shows a small distribution board with trip switches which are typically found on campsite bollards. In this instance, two 16A supplies (hook-ups) are available and are numbered 1 and 2 for identification should one trip. The sockets were also numbered 1 and 2. Circuit breakers are designed to trip if the draw of amps exceeds the breaker rating. Look again at the picture. You can see B16 printed on the two circuit breakers. Sometimes the B may be a C, but the important point is that the 16 represents 16A. This may be a 3 or a 6 with the amps respectively. The switch to the left of the circuit breakers is a residual current device (RCD). The RCD would trip if someone received an electric shock or a faulty device was used, often a kettle or a heater.

Most of Europe distributes electricity at a nominal 230V. Appliances usually have a label listing electrical specifications. Most labels show the watt value so it is worth remembering that a 16A supply provides 3,680W, whereas a 3A supply provides

The Glasgows' foolproof system.

Expect and be willing to share free electricity at Aires.

690W. The calculation is volts multiplied by amps equals watts, (230V x 16A = 3,680W). A typical domestic kettle draws approximately 2,785W at 230V, whereas a low consumption kettle can consume as little as 120W. Therefore you would need

Amps	Watts	Amps	Watts
3A	690W	10A	2,300W
5A	1,150W	13A	2,990W
6A	1,380W	16A	3,680W

over 10A supply to use a domestic kettle, but less than 3A for the low watt equivalent. Microwave ovens consume up to two times the watts at start-up, for example, a 700W microwave requires 1,400W when it starts up.

Motorhome Stopovers that offer electricity often have insufficient sockets for demand and when electricity is free it is uncommon for there to be more than one socket. Normally people share the supply, but the way this is done is potentially unsafe. Often in these situations, the circuit breakers are unavailable to the users and the supply cannot be reinstated if a circuit breaker or RCD is tripped. If you look closely at the photo above you can see one socket is shared by three motorhomes. Although this situation is less than ideal, it is fair. The photo was taken at a free French Aire and we were disappointed to see that the other end of the hook-up cable that is secured in

Multiple motorhomes sharing one plug socket.

place by silver duct tape was plugged into a UK-registered RV. Not only that, but it was parked in an area that clearly excluded motorhomes. These sockets were removed in 2014!

Continental Europeans commonly use long domestic extension cables to plug into the mains. In the UK most people use a 25m leisure cable, but 25m may not be long enough on some European campsites. Leisure cables are not designed to be driven over, but they are fitted with blue industrial plugs designed to be used outside. The blue socket identifies the source to be 230V. European campsites and Motorhome Stopovers may not have blue sockets, often providing the domestic socket of the country. A mini extension, with a leisure socket one end and a Continental two-pin plug the other, is a necessity. By attaching a domestic plug it is no longer rain proof and people often attempt to make the connection watertight by encapsulating it with a plastic bag taped with duct tape.

Reverse Polarity

Reversed polarity is the term used when the live and neutral wires are connected to the wrong terminal, i.e. live to neutral, neutral to live. This is rare in the UK, but dangerous if you tamper with any socket, switch, light fitting, or any wiring. Reverse polarity is common in France, but it is often

Camping la Manga all correct LHS. *Camping la Manga reverse polarity RHS.*

disregarded by foreign motorhomers because their electrical wiring, sockets, switches, and appliances are designed to be used with reverse polarity. Some motorhome control panels correct polarity and others have a light that identifies reversed polarity. Best practice is to test the socket before you hook-up and you can easily test polarity with a plug-in detector. These detectors also identify if an earth is present. For safety reasons, do not plug in if no earth is present. Polarity can be altered in two ways when using French or blue plugs. If you are competent, you can re-wire the plug's live and neutral on site or carry a second short extension with live and neutral wires already reversed. Reverse polarity will not damage your motorhome electrical systems, appliances,

Designed for France and Europe. Note the earth hole between the silver pins and the earth bonding strap at the bottom.

computer, or TV and you have probably used reversed polarity a few times without knowing. Europe, excluding France, has plugs that are designed to be plugged in either way around, thus it is irrelevant which way live and neutral are wired. French domestic plug sockets have a three-pin system. French plugs look virtually the same as the European plug, but the earth is connected via the hole in the plug. You do not need to worry about this as long as your mini extension plug has earth-bonding straps on the outside as well as an earth hole for France.

Solar Solutions fitting a solar panel at a motorhome show.

People intending to Offsite-Park long-term may consider fitting a solar panel. Motorhomers we have spoken to say their solar panels are able to maintain the battery at full charge during lay-up, but not when they are occupying the motorhome. The reality is you will be able to park offsite for longer, but you will not have enough power to watch TV every night. If your motorhome is stored somewhere without hook-up, then the viability of fitting a solar panel increases and may

Solar panels need an air gap to keep cool.

offset the hundreds of pounds needed to buy a solar panel system. The Achilles heel of solar panels is that they barely produce any power on inclement winter days when power is most needed by the occupants. There are different types and makes of solar panels and without individually testing them you cannot know their true performance, so do your research before you part with your cash. A solar panel fixed to the roof of a motorhome will not perform as well as advertised because the intensity of light will only be good when the sun is high in the sky. Ideally you want a moveable panel, either portable or rotating on the roof, so you can aim it toward the sun. Motorised, computer-controlled panels can track the sun, but are very expensive. The 75W solar panel seen in the photo below had been in service since 2006. The owner explained that it only worked in sunshine, though modern panels can work in overcast conditions as well. The photo was taken on the 30th of August at midday in sunny conditions and the panel was generating 4.6A of 12V electricity. The owner said that he had a solar panel fitted flat on the roof of his previous motorhome and he estimated that he would need 200W worth of roof-mounted panels to achieve the same output he was getting from his current 75W setup. He also said that 200W worth of panels would cost nearly as much as one motorised panel.

75W sun-tracking solar panel on a Dutch motorhome parked at a Stellplatz alongside the Mosel River.

The wind turbine is plane to see.

Wind turbines have similar issues to solar panels and can run in conjunction with them, but you may become a slave to electricity generation. Wind turbines start working at five knots/5.8mph and realistically will only trickle charge a battery until the wind is strong, but who wants to camp in a windy place? The biggest problem is securely fixing them. Pegging them out on the ground is difficult and contravenes the rules of setting up camp when you are entitled only to stop at the side of the road. Some people fix turbines to the rear of their motorhomes but complain they are noisy at night. Additional considerations include storage in transit and ease of erection.

Generators can recharge your on-board batteries and enable you to watch endless TV, as well as charge your electric bike or mobility scooter's batteries. American motorhomes often have large generators fitted as standard so that air conditioning can be run. European manufacturers may offer generators on the options list for some top of the range models. The reality is that few people use a generator, or at least they are rarely seen in use, because there are so few places where a responsible tourist can run one. Unsurprisingly, generator use is rarely allowed at campsites and placing a portable generator on the ground is illegal at Motorhome Stopovers or when Offsite-Parking. In addition, storage and weight for both the generator and fuel is likely to be a problem. Thankfully, there is a quiet and practical generator available as long as you have £3,000 to spend. The Telair TG480 is a LPG-fuelled generator that produces 20A. These units are chassis-mounted and probably will not be noticed when running during the day. The whole thing weighs 19kg and there is no additional fuel weight as they use the gas from the gas cylinders.

Telair TG480. Photo: Conrad Anderson.

SUPERCHARGER 50 AMP.
Photo: Ian Hamilton Cooper.

Good quality portable generators are relatively inexpensive and they command good second-hand prices. Nevertheless, before you go shopping use your motorhome for a year to see if you actually need extra power. Cheap generators are available, but as always you get what you pay for and a noisy, whiney and smoky 2-stroke generator will soon upset people around you. Even the best petrol generators are noisy if used in a quiet location and the reverberation will irritate people around you whenever you use one, therefore the less they are run the better.

According to the manufacturer, The Supercharger 50 Amp portable generator delivers a charge rate of 50A per hour. This is achieved by utilising an automotive alternator powered by a 4-stroke petrol/LPG engine. See www.thesupercharger.co.uk.

Fuel cells have the potential to provide sufficient electricity for most motorhomers. Efoy fuel cells run on highly flammable methanol which has limited availability, but 10L will be enough for weeks or possibly months. See www.efoy.com. These units are light, economical and virtually silent, but you

Efoy fuel cell and methanol fuel © SFC Energy AG.

may find it hard to justify spending £2,500 for 3.3A of electricity generation. People with a very big budget could have a Truma VeGA LPG-powered fuel cell fitted. They are compact, run on LPG and can produce 6,000W per hour at 20A. See www.conrad-anderson.co.uk for more information about the fuel cells from Efoy and Truma as well as the Telair TG480.

LED lights use between 5 to 10 times less power than tungsten filament bulbs. LED lights come in various shades of white, yellow, or green, so be sure you can try them and return if unsuitable. See www.ledbulbs4u.co.uk.

Electricity has inherent dangers. Mains electricity has sufficient energy to cause a fatality and a 12V short circuit could start a fire. We do not condone unsafe practices, nor is the previous text an installation manual. This section is merely our general comments about electricity in motorhomes. When considering carrying out any maintenance, repairs, or installations, seek professional advice. All leisure vehicles, as part of their annual service, should have the electrical systems inspected by a qualified electrician. Second-hand vehicles without supporting documentation should also have their electrical systems checked; if in doubt, always seek professional advice.

Gas

Appliances that run on gas within the motorhome typically include the fridge, hob, oven, heating and hot water systems. Often a space-efficient, combination blown-air heating and water boiler is hidden in a locker. Some motorhomes have

Cooking toast on gas is easy, simply dry fry bread in a pan.

a wall-mounted gas powered convector space heater and separate water heater. Gas is extremely flammable and can be explosive. Correct safety procedures need to be followed and regular servicing undertaken by a qualified person is advised.

There are two types of liquefied petroleum gas (LPG) used in motorhomes: butane and propane. All the appliances will work on either gas without adjustment, but the most important difference is operating temperature. Butane will remain in a liquid state at 0.5°C or below, thus cannot be used in freezing conditions. Propane can be used in temperatures as low as -42°C. Butane is also denser, and therefore heavier, than propane. For example, the bottle dimensions are identical for both Calor Gas 7kg blue butane cylinders and 6kg orange propane cylinders. The same is true for the 13kg and 15kg cylinders respectively.

There is no EU-wide agreement for gas cylinder connections. Even in the UK different connectors are required for cylinders of competing brands.

Left, German exchange gas 11kg cylinder, right a refillable cylinder.

The result is that the cylinder connections vary widely and different regulators or hose tails will be required depending where you buy a new cylinder. There is some interchange, but the easiest way is to buy the appropriate regulator or hose tail with the cylinder. Calor Gas is the market-leading brand in the UK, but there is no exchange or refill agreement outside of the UK for this or any other UK brand.

Campingaz is sold in numerous European countries, but it is impractical to use due to its small 2.75kg capacity. Since 2003 all EU-built motorhomes and caravans operate their gas systems at 30mb, early German models operated at 50mb. Gaslow sells a range of adaptors for most European cylinders.

Spanish Euro fitting and pump.

Most British motorhome gas lockers are designed to accommodate two 6/7kg Calor Gas cylinders. Most continental motorhomes accommodate two 11kg cylinders, which is a common size, but a 6/7kg and a 13/15kg Calor Gas cylinder will normally fit. If you intend to visit only one country, especially if you intend to visit the same country year after year, purchasing a foreign cylinder and appropriate attachment/regulator is cost effective and sensible.

So that an exchange can be planned, you need to know how much gas is in your cylinder. The definitive way to find out how much gas is left is to weigh the cylinder, German cylinders have weights down the side and

Big flame caused by water from the washing up draining into the burner.

Calor Gas cylinders mark the empty weight (curiously in pounds) on the aluminium collar. Externally fitted gas pressure gauges will read full until all the liquid has been turned to gas. Automatic changeover units are nice to have, but they are far from a necessity and could leave you with no reserve cylinder when topping up our refillable cylinder.

Go Motorhoming and Campervanning

The LPG that is used instead of petrol and sold at fuel stations may be a mixture of butane and propane and is suitable for motorhome gas systems. Motorhomes can have a fixed LPG gas tank fitted just like a car. For safety, these tanks have an 80 per cent cut-off valve. Filling beyond this point increases the risk of liquid propane/butane passing through the regulator. Liquid on the wrong side of the

Truma gas and 230V convector heater plus blown air, fitted in a 2015 Elddis Autoquest.

regulator is potentially catastrophic because the liquid expands approximately 250 times as it turns into a gas and the pressure is likely to cause a gas leak or significantly increased flame. With the correct adaptors it is possible to refill gas cylinders, but they must not be filled beyond 80 per cent because it is dangerous to do so. This rules out refilling Calor or any other European exchange gas cylinders. Only gas cylinders that are fitted with 80 per cent cut-off valves are designed to be refilled by the

The Cup	Denmark	**De-Visser (also known**		**Acme**	Slovakia
France	Greece	**as the Bayonet)**		Belgium	Switzerland
Italy	Hungary	United Kingdom		Germany	
Portugal	Turkey	The Netherlands		Ireland	
Austria	Croatia	Norway		Luxembourg	
Switzerland	Sweden			Poland	

general public. You can buy refillable gas cylinders from Gaslow, www.gaslowdirect.com, Tel: 0845 4000600, and Autogas 2000 who supply lightweight aluminium cylinders, visit www.autogas.co.uk, Tel: 01845 523 213. Refillable gas cylinders eliminate rental cylinder exchange problems and adaptor/hose tail incompatibility. Filling up with LPG from fuel stations is also much cheaper than exchanging a Calor Gas cylinder. When you come to sell your motorhome, simply keep your refillable cylinder or sell it separately. Refillable cylinders fitted with a float gauge rather than a pressure gauge are preferable, but the secret is to refill before the gas level becomes low; they can be topped up at any point.

The gas from two 11kg gas cylinders was all that was required during six months wintering at a UK campsite because gas was required for cooking only. The campsite's showers, a laundry and electric hook-up were used. The caravan's water heater and fridge ran on electricity and an electric fan heater and kettle were used.

During a one-month ski tour in temperatures ranging from 0°C to 21°C, without electric hook-up, we used the gas from one 11kg cylinder per week. In these temperatures a refillable cylinder and a spare cylinder is the most convenient option.

Both of our Pilotes were fitted with identical under-worktop Thetford fridge-freezers. They worked extremely well, but both would consume all the gas from one 11kg cylinder per pitched week during summer.

LPG Availability

There should be no problem filling a fixed tank abroad, but a refillable gas cylinder may be refused especially if it is taken out of the motorhome locker. We recommend that you fit an external filler point for your refillable cylinders to prevent any problems. In our experience if you are turned away at one fuel station the next will probably welcome your trade, but it helps if you have the correct filling attachment connected before you get to the fuel station. The three main filling adapters are shown in the picture opposite.

LPG is difficult to obtain in parts of Europe. LPG availability is detailed in the *All the Aires* guides and online at www.go-motorhoming.co.uk. Country specific websites include: stations.gpl.online.fr (France), www.volvo200.org/lpg.htm (Sweden), and www.gjelstenli.no/lpg (Norway).

Safety

Gas is highly flammable. Gas cylinders should always be turned off in transit unless an appropriate safety regulator is fitted. Vents in the floor of the gas locker must never be covered or blocked with mud or snow. Gas cylinders must be transported and used in a secure upright position as liquid butane/propane could pass through the regulator resulting in a very big flame. Suspected gas leaks should always be investigated fully using soapy water before appliances are used. Rinse off any soap to prevent corrosion. Gas leaks on ferries are potentially catastrophic because gas sinks to the lowest point creating a potentially explosive atmosphere. Therefore gas systems should be turned off before embarkation. All leisure vehicles, as part of their annual service, should have the systems inspected by a qualified LPG engineer.

Water Systems

Motorhomes can have three separate systems: fresh water, dirty water from sinks and showers called waste water/grey water, and toilet waste called black waste water.

Motorhomes generally have a fixed freshwater tank, normally located internally; smaller Van Conversions often have one or two refillable plastic canisters. A secure internal fresh tank is preferable when Offsite-Parking and essential in sustained freezing conditions. A tank that holds less than 100L is insufficient when Offsite-Parking. When staying on campsites it is nice to have a water tank that does not need filling daily, but fully serviced pitches that provide constant fresh water are becoming more common.

Water is heavy, 1L weighs 1kg, and to stay within the motorhome's weight limits it may be necessary to discard fresh water before departing. This is fine if you know exactly where you are going, but inadvisable if you don't. Ideally you should travel with sufficient water for one night, just in case.

Two 12L water bottles fitted in a Concept Multi Car Reimo Van Conversion.

On average, two adults experienced in Offsite-Parking use 20L of water per day for drinks, washing up and other essentials. Showering uses up to 15L per person, possibly more if long hair is washed. 5L is plenty for a strip wash. Washing clothes uses 20L of water. With strict water conservation it is possible to use less than 20L per day, but it is far easier to use 100L or more. Four nights is the longest we have stopped away from a water supply and we still had 30L left in our 110L tank.

Always ask if water is available wherever you stop and when gathering Offsite-Parking information from other motorhomers. People using

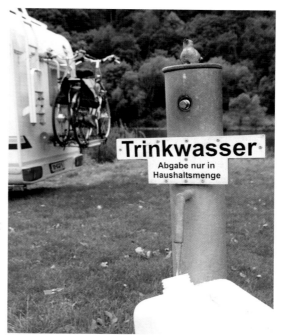

Drinking water tap at Ediger Burg Stellplatz alongside the Mosel River in Germany.

Motorhome Stopovers and Offsite-Parking on an 'as we find them' basis generally travel with water tanks at least three quarters full making it possible to stay a few days wherever they may find themselves. Many experienced Offsite-Parking motorhomers carry a full tank of water and additional water in containers at the expense of other items.

There are several ways to fill motorhome water tanks. Motorhomes with internal or under-slung water tanks normally have an outside filler point, which looks similar to a fuel cap. Many campsites and Motorhome Stopovers have areas designed for motorhomes to discharge and restock with water. A short length of food-quality hose is useful, but you will also need various tap connections. Water tanks located under seats or between floor layers usually have a large inspection/filler hole making filling easy. We almost exclusively fill up the tank through the inspection/filler hole and use a 20L plastic water bottle to transport the water from the tap. Plastic watering cans are popular for keeping tanks topped up. Whatever you intend to use, ensure it is food quality as plastic items, especially hoses, can cause water to take on a chemical taste similar to the antiseptic TCP.

Go Motorhoming and Campervanning

Water quality varies across Europe and can appear a little dubious, even when marked 'potable'. Bottled drinking water is cheap and widely available but it is costly on space, weight, and convenience. Drinking water is available in campsites. Public water taps may be found in town squares. Look for 'potable' signs, sometimes the only identifier is seeing other people filling water bottles. Water may have a cloudy

CAK waste trap and Nature Pure water filter.

appearance or a chemical taste. Water purification tablets or liquids can be used if you have concerns about water-borne bacteria. A water filter is most convenient and they are relatively easy to fit. Some water filters are designed to improve clarity, smell, and taste, but you actually need to install a water filter that eliminates bacteria as well as nasty tastes. Replacement filter cartridges may need to be carried if you intend to travel for six months or more.

As discussed in the gas section, a gas powered water heater is likely to be fitted inside a cupboard. 10-15L of hot water is heated in about half an hour. Some water heaters also have a 230V heat element. It may be possible to retrofit an electric element, but it is unlikely to be cost effective except for people that regularly winter in their motorhomes. Most people get by with boiling a kettle and using the shower blocks.

Truma combination water heater fitted in our Cityvan.

Summer campers can make use of a solar shower. This is a black plastic sack with a shower head coming off it. Basically, you fill it with water and leave it out in the sun all day to heat up. On very hot days the water can get too hot and cold water will need to be added before use. Please remember, when Offsite-Parking and using Motorhome Stopovers it is illegal to set up camp.

Waste water, commonly called grey water, refers to dirty water from sinks and showers. Waste water is either collected in a fixed tank mounted under the floor or an outside portable container. Motorhomers wishing to Offsite-Park or use Motorhome Stopovers must have a motorhome with a fixed tank. It is common practice for a fixed waste water tank to be 10 per cent smaller than the freshwater tank. Fixed waste water tanks are one of the few disadvantages of staying on campsites in a motorhome because it is inconvenient to pack up and move just to empty waste tanks. To overcome this problem you can use an empty toilet cassette for transporting waste water; curiously, waste water leaves a smell that cannot be rinsed away. Campsite staff and subsequent campers get upset if they find a pile of food waste, which inevitably collects when waste water is drained on pitch rather than in the facility provided. Campsites that do not have a motorhome Service Point sometimes have a drain cover that can be lifted, but it is best to ask upon arrival.

Benicassim motorhome Service Point in Spain.

Chris emptying a toilet tank at Dudelange Aire, Luxembourg.

Disposing of waste water is easy at a motorhome Service Point, but carry a short length of hose to direct the water directly to the drain. Draining your waste tanks anywhere other than at an official place is likely to be illegal and harmful to the environment because of the chemicals and surfactants. Some motorhome manufacturers seem unaware that it is essential that waste tanks completely drain to prevent an unpleasant smell building up. Snail-trails of waste water are commonly seen on roads near motorhome Service Points, and this is likely to upset local residents. People intentionally leave drain taps open and it may be necessary to go up and down steep hills and round tight bends to completely empty the tank. Tank smells are inevitable during hot weather, but you can reduce this by restricting the volume of bacteria friendly liquids such as oils, starchy water, and washing up water. Pouring diluted bicarbonate of soda occasionally down the drains helps to keep the tank clean and reduces smells; proprietary products are available. You could fit a waste trap to the drainage pipe under the sink and an example can be seen in the water filter picture on page 82. External tank contents will freeze in sustained freezing conditions. See Wintering in Chapter 4.

Toilet waste, commonly called black water, must be disposed of responsibly as it poses a health risk. Emptying toilet cassettes into public toilets is generally unacceptable because it is almost impossible to empty a toilet cassette into a toilet without making a mess. Furthermore, it is probably illegal and will almost certainly upset local residents.

Motorhomes such as American RVs with fixed toilet waste tanks have to be driven to the Service Point unless on a suitably serviced pitch. When plumbed into an on-pitch waste system the tank must still be used and emptied periodically. Leaving the drain valve open will result in a build up of solids in the tank. Attempting to drain a fixed toilet tank into a bucket will almost certainly result in an agricultural outcome and is definitely antisocial for neighbours. Most Motorhome Stopovers have a waste drain, but access and use may be a problem.

There are several variations on how toilets flush. Our least favourite automatically flushes when you open the

RV draining toilet then wastewater at Calais.

waste hole and it may be necessary to turn off the water pump in certain situations. Some toilets have a flushing reservoir and toilet flush chemical can be added, but the tanks are prone to growing algae that then sticks to the bowl when the flush is activated. Some toilet flush systems are directly fed from the onboard water supply. This is a curious arrangement because water bylaws state, in domestic and industrial situations, that fresh water systems must not be able to siphon contaminated water. For instance, household toilets have a cistern to ensure that drinking water cannot become contaminated. We strongly recommend that you make up a spray bottle of toilet flush solution and spray both the toilet bowl and flush exit every time you use the toilet.

Potty training is a necessary subject. When you want a number two there are some things you must do. Wet the bowl by flush or spray and place toilet paper around the exit hole. If you keep the hole open during proceedings, and you have good aim, the bowl will stay clean. It is worth scrunching up some toilet paper and dropping it down the hole first to reduce the risk of splashing.

Chemicals may be used in portable toilet cassettes. Traditionally the chemicals were blue and these normally contain biocides which kill bacteria in the tank and control smells. Remotely located campsites often have septic tank waste systems which cannot cope with biocides. Using environmentally friendly 'green' chemicals or a SOG system are suitable alternatives. SOG is a brand name for a simple extraction system designed for built-in cassette-style toilets. These extraction systems are more efficient at controlling toileting smells than proprietary chemicals because a constant airflow is drawn through the toilet bowl. This is very welcome in a small space, especially when sharing the motorhome with less than

Go Motorhoming and Campervanning

intimate friends. Fitting a SOG system is relatively easy if you have basic 12V electrical knowledge and contortionist arms. SOG systems are definitely good value for money and we consider them essential. This ultimate environmentally friendly system cuts out the weight, space, cost, and need of chemicals.

SOG toilet extractor fan being fitted at a show.

Concentrated blue chemical also stains everything it comes in contact with. The only negative of a SOG system is vented smells may be directed to your neighbours or 'worse still' into your awning; however, chimney systems are available. Visit www.soguk.co.uk, Tel: 0845 8698940.

When touring, discharge waste water and toilet waste at every opportunity, regardless of tank levels, as your next stop may not have facilities. Some campsites charge you for servicing if you only stay one night, so always read the small print.

All motorhomers represent the motorhoming community. Offsite-Parking motorhomers need to be particularly responsible, especially when it comes to the disposal of toilet waste. Dumping a toilet full of chemicals and waste in the countryside is environmentally unfriendly, unnecessary, and probably against the law everywhere. It is not always possible to dispose of waste as regularly as you would like, the following options all have their merits.

Two toilet cassettes: Carrying a spare toilet cassette in an outside locker is favoured by German motorhomers. Cassettes are relatively expensive, bulky and weigh about 20kg when full. Fiamma produce a Porta Kassett designed to carry a spare toilet cassette underneath the motorhome.

Liquids only: Limiting toilet use to urine only, not even toilet paper, will increase the time before emptying and the emptying experience is less hideous. We know one couple that use their toilet for solids only when offsite parking in remote locations. Thankfully we have never ended up at the disposal point at the same time. Public toilets or the bag technique (see text in blue) can also be used to deal with solid waste.

Toilet emptying and water collection at Ouistreham Aire, France.

Warning! The following text in blue contains the realities some people will not want to know, so if you are not going to Offsite-Park, move on to Chapter 4.

The bottle technique: Men can refill lidded bottles and discard the waste in a bin or down a toilet when available. Plastic fabric conditioner bottles with wide necks are worth saving.

The bag technique: Use bags for your solid waste including toilet tissue. Incidentally, bags specially designed to hold in place in Thetford toilet bowls are available in German camping shops. Carrier bags work well, but always check for holes! We recommend having a pee before attempting this procedure and advise that toilet paper is put in the bag first, just in case. Disposal in communal wheelie bins, which are commonly available all over Europe, ensures waste is safely disposed of as these bins are also used for nappies and sanitary wear. When immediate disposal is not possible, the bag can be stored in an airtight jar; sauerkraut jars are particularly suitable. Some people have not worked out responsible toileting and disappear into the bushes with a roll of toilet paper, charming!

Vicarious Shop

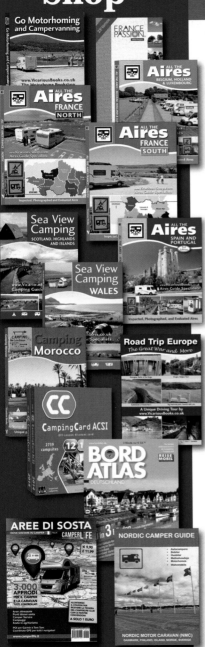

CHAPTER 4 – Preparing Your Motorhome

There are more gadgets and gismos available than you can shake a stick at. The reality is that the payloads on many motorhomes will not allow for more than the essentials. You may have to make tough decisions such as: do you install satellite TV or save the weight so that you can keep your booze cupboard stocked up?

Essential Items

There is an ever changing list of items that you are required to carry in your motorhome when travelling in Europe. We recommend that you visit the AA's website (www.theaa.com) to see the latest requirements.

Bare Necessities

Legal or strongly recommended
Headlamp modifiers
GB sticker/GB number plates
High visibility vests
Two pairs of driving glasses, if needed
Two NF-registered breathalysers (France)
Spare bulb and fuse kits
Fire extinguisher
Two red warning triangles
First aid kit
Spare wheel or repair kit

Administration
Original registration document
Insurance documents
Money and credit/debit cards
Passport(s)/visa(s)
Safety and security
Smoke alarm
Carbon monoxide alarm
Safe or strongbox
Recommended
Torch

Some motorhomers keep high visibility vests on the front seatbacks. They look ugly, but this is a good idea because you are likely to need them in a hurry and some countries require vests to be worn as soon as you exit the vehicle onto the roadside. Some countries require warning triangles to be easily accessible from within the vehicle, again a good idea. A fire extinguisher may be a requirement of your vehicle insurance. An AFFF foam 1L extinguisher costs less than £25, surely a wise investment! The initials of the country where the vehicle is registered must be displayed when driving on the Continent. Euro number plates display the country initials in a blue box on the left-hand side and are accepted within the EU. A national decal will be required if no Euro plates are fitted or when travelling outside the EU. Right-hand-drive headlights must be modified so they do not dazzle oncoming drivers. Applying headlight modifiers is easy, but you need to be able to see the beam pattern. Shining the headlights onto a wall at night is best. You need to flatten the pattern by eliminating the kick ups on the left-hand sides. We recommend carrying at least one spare set of headlight modifiers in case of loss or damage.

Security

Crime involving motorhomes is low, but you can greatly reduce the risks by not stopping at motorway services, day or night. Road crime hotspots include the main routes through southern France and Spain. Thieves also target unattended motorhomes in supermarket car parks. Campsites may seem like safe havens, but petty theft is common especially at campsites near capital cities. We recommend that you be as vigilant at campsites as you would when Offsite-Parking. No matter where you are always lock up when you leave your motorhome unattended, even for just a minute whilst you pop to the loo.

Criminals like easy targets and most motorhomes may as well have an enormous bullseye painted on the outside. Plastic roof vents and plastic windows secured with plastic catches can often be pulled open by hand, but are easy to prise open with a crowbar. That said, the caravan (habitation area) door is the most likely place for a thief to try and force open. Exterior opening lockers are also vulnerable. Cab doors that can be unlocked with an electronic key fob offer no security against digital entry devices. The same devices can also program ignition keys to suit the individual vehicle.

We strongly recommend that you fit additional locks to all the doors on your motorhome. Locks are available in several styles from strong deadlocks to lockable grab handles. Fiamma and Milenco produce deadlocks suitable for the caravan doors. To prevent being locked in, ensure that you choose locks that allow you to operate them from inside and outside. There are several types of additional or replacement locks for cab doors, just search for van locks online. Cab doors can be held shut by passing a ratchet strap through the handles, it may also be possible to secure doors with the seatbelts (see photo). Fitting a steering wheel lock is necessary on vehicles with keyless ignition and recommended in general. Sliding window security is improved by cutting a dowel to fit into the bottom channel, thereby jamming the window. Covering fixed ladders prevents easy

This Autocruise has a double latch system, but often only one latch is located at the middle of the frame.

access to vulnerable skylights. Outside sensor lights are convenient for you and could disturb a potential thief or make you aware that something has come close to the motorhome. Audible sensors are also available.

Integrated alarms, immobilisers, and trackers provide peace of mind and may attract discounts against insurance fees. Immobilisers have been mandatory on new cars since 1998 and most ignition systems now require the correctly coded ignition key to start the engine, thus making hot wiring a thing of the past. Commercial Vehicle manufacturers phased in immobilisers as standard between 1998 and 2002, but, taking into account late conversion or registration, 2004/5 motorhomes may not have an immobiliser. Immobilisers fitted post manufacture also prevent the engine from starting and may be integrated with an alarm system. Often an electronic key fob is used to arm and disarm the system. However, if you attach this to your keys and they are stolen, the security advantage is lost. Some immobilisers utilise a Radio Frequency Device (RFD), which allows the engine to start as long as the device is inside the vehicle. Often the RFD is credit card-sized, making it convenient to carry in a wallet or purse.

The following data was provided by Thatcham Research in May 2013: *'Depending on where you live in the UK and which vehicle you drive, the chances of getting your vehicle recovered are low and decreasing, given that a large amount of vehicle theft is now attributed to international, organised gangs who will very quickly aim to get your vehicle out of the country and most likely strip it for parts. However, if you have a Thatcham Category 6 stolen vehicle tracking system fitted the chances of recovery increase to 65-70%. With a Category 5 system which automatically tracks unauthorised movement of your vehicle and alerts the relevant authorities your chances of recovery rise to around 99%.'*

Put the seatbelt through the door handle to hold the door shut. Also note the steering lock.

UK Towbars Ltd custom build strong storage boxes, www.uk-towbars.net.

Alarms sounding are so common that most people ignore them; therefore unmonitored alarms are only useful if you are within earshot. Some alarm systems send messages to data centres who in turn contact named persons should an event occur that requires attention. Other alarm systems send messages to personal telephones to notify the recipient of a given event. In our opinion, this level of contact is necessary as we previously had an unmonitored alarm that regularly went off without our knowing.

Our Cobra Alarm was unintentionally set off at least once a day when the key fob is carried in a pocket.

Alarm systems designed for motorhomes monitor the doors and lockers and have an internal movement sensor. The most reassuring feature is the perimeter alarm and this is something we use at night both on and off campsites. When you select the perimeter setting the internal sensor is not activated, so people and pets are able to move around inside whilst the doors and lockers are monitored. Always check the alarm key fob carefully before committing to an alarm as bad design can lead to frustration when the 'panic' alarm is constantly triggered from your pocket.

Vehicle trackers should reduce the time taken by police to recover a stolen vehicle. Hopefully the criminals will be caught and any insurance claim settled quicker. Cars stolen by professionals in the UK are more likely to be stripped into parts than resold, so the first five hours from theft are critical for recovery. Trackers operate in different ways and provide varying levels of service. Ensure that there is an adequate level of service across Europe and confirm who liaises with the local police. Trackers can be self-installed for less than the cost of a one-year subscription for a branded product. These inexpensive trackers are self-monitored via a mobile phone SIM card. Some have the ability to disable the 12V and fuel systems.

Choosing the correct alarm or tracker is complicated and thorough research will be necessary. Purchasing a system that has been tested by an independent body should prevent you from making a bad purchase. There are two key UK companies: Thatcham and Sold Secure. The Motor Insurance Repair Research Centre, known as Thatcham, rates alarms, immobilisers and trackers in categories from 1-7 (1 being the most complex) and a full list of approved devices with appropriate contact details is available on their website, www.thatcham.org, Tel: 01635 868855.

The device may also have been tested by Sold Secure and a searchable database of approved products is available on their website, www.soldsecure.com, Tel: 01327 264687.

Alarms and trackers can be fitted by most motorhome dealers and by alarm and tracker specialists. Our Aventura has an Outsmart the Thief system which we have been using for two years and would readily recommend, see www.606060.com. Additional security can be purchased at motorhome dealers, motorhome shows, and online.

Every year Vicarious Media receives two or three phone calls from customers who have had their motorhomes broken into. The common theme is that no additional physical security was in use and that the valuable items taken were not secured in a safe. Often just a briefcase or bag has been taken, sometimes all the cupboards have been rifled. The simple rule is: if you do not want to lose it, do not take it with you. Important documents have to be taken with you and should be stored securely. No system is foolproof and delaying a determined thief or negating an opportunist situation is probably the most you can achieve. Small, reasonably light safes are available from DIY superstores and Argos. It is hard to get a good fixing in a motorhome, so choose a safe that you can fit into the floor well or a cupboard. Laptop safes with enough space for all essentials are also worth considering.

Security does not finish with physical deterrents, common sense or simple tricks of the mind are just as important. A good example is sticking multi language labels on windows explaining that a sophisticated alarm is fitted.

Every time you park consider the following:
• Park in a visible and illuminated space rather than an isolated dark corner.
• Keep your valuables out of sight, preferably in a safe.
• When you go to bed leave a 'mugger's wallet' out on the side so your real one is not searched for (see page 167).
• Tie a dog lead on your bike rack or leave a pair of size 12 gents' shoes under the step.
• When you go out shut the curtains and blinds and leave a light or radio on so that people assume the motorhome is occupied.
• Never leave keys lying around or on display at any time.

Safety

Smoke alarms designed for caravans are less prone to going off when you burn the toast and often have a temporary silence function. They cost around £20 and it would be silly not to have one. Likewise, a carbon monoxide alarm should be considered essential. Carbon monoxide is an odourless, colourless, and tasteless gas which is produced when burning fossil fuels, such as LPG, ineffectively. Initially carbon monoxide is undetectable to humans and mild levels will cause early symptoms of poisoning like light-headedness, confusion, headaches, vertigo, and flu-like effects. When the concentration is above 100 parts per million it is highly toxic if enough is inhaled. Motorhomes generally have gas cookers, heating, and hot water systems, all of which can produce carbon monoxide. Ensure that the annual habitation service engineer tests these items sufficiently. Each time you go away in your motorhome test that the smoke and carbon monoxide alarms are working. The FireAngel ST-

This alarm displays the actual level of carbon monoxide but others have an audible alarm only.

Following repairs our fridge leaked exhaust gasses containing carbon monoxide into the motorhome. This was easily fixed by securing the top baffle.

620 Thermoptek™ smoke alarm is NCC approved and has a 10-year battery, see http://fireangel.co.uk.

Gas alarms are devices that detect LPG gas leaks and the anaesthetic gasses alleged to be used in burglaries. Gas alarms have sold very well due to the fear of 'Gas Attacks'. Increased use is a good thing because a gas leak is infinitely more likely than criminals trying to render occupants of vehicles unconscious by spraying in highly flammable gasses. Gas attacks are reportedly happening at motorway service areas when vehicles are broken into. The Royal College of Anaesthetists released the following statement in 2007, and confirmed they still stand by the statement in 2014:

'It is the view of the College [of Anaesthetists] that it would not be possible to render someone unconscious by blowing ether, chloroform or any of the currently used volatile anaesthetic agents, through the window of a motor-home without their knowledge, even if they were sleeping at the time. Ether is an extremely pungent agent and a relatively weak anaesthetic by modern standards and has a very irritant affect on the air passages, causing coughing and sometimes vomiting. It takes some time to reach unconsciousness, even if given by direct application to the face on a cloth, and the concentration needed by some sort of spray administered directly into a room would be enormous. The smell hangs around for days and would be obvious to anyone the next day. Even the more powerful modern volatile agents would need to be delivered in tanker loads of carrier gas by a large compressor...

The other important point to remember is that general anaesthetics are potentially very dangerous, which is why they are only administered in the UK by doctors who have undergone many years of postgraduate training in the subject and who remain with the unconscious patient throughout the anaesthetic...

If there was a totally safe, odourless, potent, cheap anaesthetic agent available to thieves for this purpose it is likely the medical profession would know about it and be investigating its use in anaesthetic practice.'

We have spoken to 12 couples that have had their motorhomes broken into whilst stopping at motorway rest areas. Some of the people woke up, others could not believe they could sleep through a robbery, and two couples assumed they must have been gassed. It is a strange thing that people often sleep through domestic burglary yet no one assumes they have been gassed. The reality is that motorway service stations and parking areas are busy, noisy, transient places and the thieves are professional. To our knowledge no victims who believe they were gassed have been blood tested to prove that anaesthetic was inhaled, nor have there been any reported deaths or reports of motorhomes exploding because they were filled with highly-flammable anaesthetic gas. If you have bona fide evidence to the contrary, please let us know.

Remember that everything we do in life involves an element of risk. The best way to avoid the risk of burglary is simply to never stop overnight at motorway service or rest areas, instead stay at a local campsite or Motorhome Stopover. Do not drive until you are too exhausted to make sensible decisions. Plan long drives with an hour break every four hours and do not drive for more than eight hours per day. When travelling with children, reduce driving times and take more breaks. Whenever you park somewhere where you feel there is a risk of crime, set your motorhome's alarm and keep doors and windows shut and locked and valuables secured in a safe.

Driving Safety And Comfort

On average, UK Coachbuilt motorhomes travel 3,700 miles per year. However, the tyres are capable of covering 40,000+ miles and it is very common to see the original tyres on quite old motorhomes. The compounds that tyres are made of naturally degrade with age, especially when exposed to strong sunlight, and tyres over five years old may well need replacing irrespective of tread depth. This photo taken in April 2010 shows the sidewall of an ageing tyre fitted to a motorhome that was for sale. The number 1501 identifies the manufacture date to be week 15, year 2001. Make a routine inspection of your tyres each time you go away in your motorhome. Check the overall condition, tread depth, look for cracking, and check the tyre pressures. Since motorhomes are always fully laden, tyre pressures need to be higher than you might expect or even higher than that advised by the

The cracking on this nine-year-old tyre leaves no doubt that it should be replaced.

chassis manufacturer. The motorhome handbook should display the correct tyre pressures, but if there is any doubt contact the motorhome manufacturer. Some people cover the tyres to protect them from the sun and this may be worth doing when parked up for a long time. It is important to change the resting position of the tyres and we recommend that you drive the motorhome fortnightly to keep the engine lubricated and guarantee a new resting point for the tyres.

Michelin, Pirelli, and Continental tyre manufacturers have designed tyres specifically for heavily laden motorhomes, the main feature being extra sidewall reinforcement. They are often referred to as camping tyres, but are correctly identified by the letters CP; standard van tyres are only marked with a C. New motorhomes not built upon motorhome-specific chassis often have C classification tyres fitted. We have used "camping tyres" manufactured by Michelin, Pirelli and Vanco Continental. All performed well in wet and dry conditions, gripping to the road under heavy braking and when driving faster than most motorhome users would on mountain roads. Overall we prefer Michelin camping tyres, but find that they wear quicker than Vancos. If you are likely to encounter snow on your trip, consider fitting mud and snow tyres which are designed to provide more grip in icy conditions. Mud and snow tyres are identified by an 'M+S', or a mountain or snowflake symbol.

Winter tyres are often marked M+S.

A reversing camera system should be high on your wish list and should be selected when you are filling out a sales order for a new motorhome. You are most likely to damage your motorhome when manoeuvring at very slow speeds and any visual advantage you can give yourself is worth having. Little dents and scrapes on motorhome bodywork are expensive to repair and may require the whole panel to be replaced to do a proper job. The armed forces train their logistics personnel on how to give and to react to reversing commands. Military drivers are trained not to look in their mirrors when receiving directions from a banksman who remains at the front of the vehicle during the entire reverse manoeuvre. We have never seen this done by motorhome couples, but have seen plenty of comical situations with communication breakdown. We recommend that you agree your manoeuvring communication signals, then take your motorhome to a large empty car park or field and practice common manoeuvring situations. Reversing camera systems are multi-function: they can automatically switch on when reverse gear is selected; whilst driving, they can be used to view trailers or traffic behind you; when parked, they can be used as a security device enabling you to see and hear what is happening outside; and the monitor can also double as a TV. Ensure that the reversing camera is positioned so that you can reach it from the ground because the lens needs regular cleaning in wet conditions and they also suffer from condensation. You will become reliant upon your reversing camera, though you will not realise how much unless it breaks down.

Suspension enhancement is not necessary on a well-designed and correctly loaded motorhome. Fitting an air suspension aid to a motorhome significantly improves ride comfort when the motorhome is very wide, tall or has a large overhang; it should prevent the feeling of a boat at sea. Ensure that load and brake-monitoring systems will not be affected before fitting because altering the ride height could cause any load-sensing device to provide unbalanced front and rear braking. Whether it is worth adding suspension aids is purely down to cost against use during ownership, but should not be added to facilitate overloading. For further information visit www.airide.co.uk, Tel: 07961 251359, www.as-airsuspension.co.uk, Tel: 01925 740666 and www.vbairsuspension.co.uk.

Get Lost

When we were Full-Timing our outlook was: How can you get lost when you don't know where you are going? Oh, how things change. Now that we have entered the satellite age, you may think that maps are pointless. The reality is maps are as important as ever because motorhoming is as much about the journey as the destination. Blindly following your satellite navigator will take you along main roads and motorways, missing out scenic routes or sites of interest along the way. Like most people, we use a satellite navigator when we are driving on unfamiliar roads, but unless we are driving alone, the sound is muted and the satellite navigator is used only as an aid alongside map navigation.

Advanced route planning allows you to study your maps and consider your preferred routes. Maps normally detail scenic routes, thermal waters,

Are you taking the GPS?

viewpoints, and places of interest, many of which will not be found in guidebooks. You cannot rely on buying good maps as you enter a country, so investigate and purchase the maps you need before you leave the UK. Vicarious Shop offers popular European maps and Stanfords has a big range of maps available in store or online at www.stanfords.co.uk, Tel: 020 78361321. Strange as it may seem, European maps can be written in English; we once drove past Wien in Austria when we fully intended to visit Vienna as printed on our map. We still have not been to Wien (Vienna). You need to be able to navigate minor roads, so you need maps at a scale no more than 1:400,000. Europe-wide road atlases do not go down to this scale, so you will need to buy country specific maps and/or atlases. Road atlases are easiest to use when in transit, whereas foldout maps are good for route planning. A Europe-wide map is essential when information sharing with other motorhomers. Write the information you gather directly onto the map, that way you will come across it if you decide to travel in that area or country again.

There are many different satellite navigation devices available. Until now, our opinion was that you get what you pay for, but in this case it does not seem necessary to spend a lot of money. A handheld satellite navigator can be used when away from your motorhome, which is an enormous advantage compared to a fixed installation. Over the past seven years we have tested and used six different models and brands of satellite navigator and can confirm that they all navigated us to our destination most of the time, although they do sometimes get lost. They all tried to navigate us down unmade tracks, and sometimes did not have roads that had clearly been there for decades. All suggested farcical routes, such as driving many miles in the wrong direction to a motorway junction when we were already on a perfectly good road travelling in the correct direction. 'Satnaff special shortcuts' are our favourite, some are so crazy you ask yourself who programs these things. That said, we consider a satellite navigator an essential item and carry two in case one breaks down. We rely heavily on our satellite navigator in large towns when we are trying to find somewhere in a backstreet, and they come into their own when used in conjunction with accurate GPS coordinates. Nearly all the destination guides sold on the Vicarious Shop have GPS coordinates for each place listed and, for that reason, we strongly recommend you buy a satellite navigator that does take coordinates.

There are two ways to program a satellite navigator to locate a specified place, either by typing in an address or a coordinate. Typing in postcodes works well in the UK where they are street specific, but European postcodes will often cover an entire town and its surroundings. When you want to pinpoint an exact location you need a coordinate; to complicate this there are three commonly used coordinate types:

• Degrees, Minutes & Seconds, written as: N51°04'53.88" E001°10'58.92"
• Degree Decimal Minutes, written as: N51°04.898' E1°10.982'
• Decimal Degrees, written as: N51.081639° E1.183031°

Guidebooks may use any one of the above types of coordinate, for example Vicarious Media uses the Degree Decimal Minutes format (N51°04.898' E001°10.982'), so ensure your device accepts all three formats.

The Prime Meridian runs through Greenwich, London and measures 0°. Meridians are measured up to 180° east or west of the Prime Meridian and represent longitude on the globe. The equator, at 0°, represents the centre of the earth from the north and south poles and the latitudinal lines known as parallels are measured up to 90° north and south of the equator. In order to pinpoint a position, each set of coordinates, no matter which type, has two parts. Each part is a collection of numbers and symbols behind a letter; either N or S depending if you are north or south of the equator, and E or W depending whether you are east or west of the Prime Meridian line. If no letters are displayed, then west is indicated as a negative figure (i.e. -10.1234°).

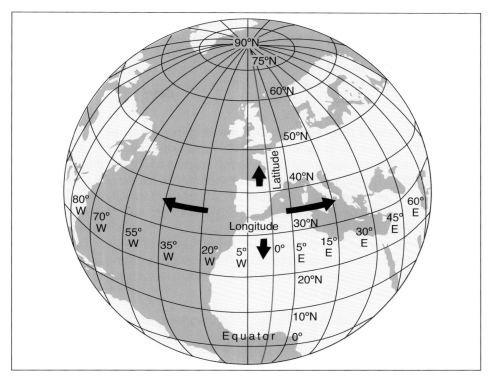

Meridians and parallels – the basis of measuring time, distance and direction.

Ken Rowley explains how to convert the different types of coordinates:

Decimal Degrees are usually given to four or five decimal places. For example, a coordinate with four decimal places (i.e. 10.1234) has an accuracy of 36.4'. Five decimal places (i.e. 10.12345) improves the accuracy to 3.64', just less than 3'8". Degree Decimal Minutes are often given to three decimal places (i.e. 10°12.345') which gives an accuracy of just over 6'; close enough to be acceptable for most people's needs.

The maths required to change between the formats is not complicated and can be readily achieved using a basic calculator. The compass direction at the beginning of each coordinate does not change. The degrees value does not change; this is the number between the compass direction (N, S, E, or W) and the first punctuation (either a degrees symbol or a full stop). For clarification, the underlined text on the following coordinates stays the same: N10°12.345', N10.12345°, N10°12'20.7".

Changing Degree Decimal Minutes into Decimal Degrees. *To convert N10°12.345', ignore for now the degrees value (see above) and divide the minutes, everything after the degree symbol, by 60. In the example N10°12.345', the minutes (12.345) are divided by 60 = 0.20575. Add the degrees value and directional letter (N10°) to the front of the new decimal (.20575) and the answer is N10.20575°.*

Changing Decimal Degrees into Degree Decimal Minutes. *To convert N10.12345°, ignore the degrees value (see above) and consider the decimal part of the degrees, everything past the full stop (.12345). Multiply 0.12345 by 60 = 7.407'. The number to the left of the decimal point (which may be one or two digits) represents the minutes, while the decimal number to the right of the decimal point shows the decimal minutes. Add the degrees value and directional letter and the conversion is N10°7.407' minutes. To avoid possible confusion, minutes are always specified by two digits before the decimal point. This means that 7.407' minutes is written (and entered into your satellite navigator) as 07.407'. So the answer above is correctly given in the form N10°07.407'.*

Changing Degree Decimal Minutes into Degrees, Minutes and Seconds. *To convert N10°12.345', simply multiply the seconds, the very last part of the coordinate, by 60. Ignore the N10°12 and multiply .345 by 60 = 20.7. The 20.7 is added to the end of the N10°12' to make N10°12'20.7". To convert Degrees, Minutes and Seconds into Degree Decimal Minutes, simply divide the 20.7" by 60.*

Both parts of the coordinate must be converted and it is imperative the correct letter is assigned to each part and the decimal point is put in the correct place. However, when choosing a satellite navigator I would strongly recommend that you buy one that takes all three coordinate types. It makes life much simpler!

When you buy your satellite navigator, ensure you find out where you input the GPS coordinates and which types it can take. Do not take a sales representative's word that the machine accepts coordinates. Both TomTom and Garmin produce some satellite navigators that accept all three types of coordinates. We recommend that you test the three different types of coordinates to make sure the satellite navigator identifies the correct location, the following coordinates all locate Vicarious Shop on Tontine Street in Folkestone: N51.081639° E001.183031° or N51°04'53.88" E001°10'58.92" or N51°04.898' E001°10.982'. You must enter every symbol when you enter the coordinates.

Satellite navigators are easy to use as long as you read the handbook, even technophobes should cope. The satellite navigator will be set to its default settings when you take it out of the box and you may wish to change some settings to suit your preferences. Often you can choose to avoid toll roads or choose the shortest route, the fastest route or main routes. If you select 'fastest route' the satellite navigator will select country lanes with a national speed limit of 60mph over main routes restricted to 40mph. If you select 'shortest route' the routes are likely to include narrow country lanes; we have been directed to drive off-road down green lanes. No doubt programmers will address these issues in time.

Before you drive off blindly following your satellite navigator's instructions, select your destination and preview the chosen route. Even 20-something Full-Timers George and Kate (see page II) fell foul by driving to Bingen in Germany only to discover after two hours of driving that they were in the wrong province. You may have to input some 'via points' at strategic junctions if you want to make the satellite navigator choose specific roads. When you are underway and the satellite navigator directs you to turn off, always assess the road before turning into it and be prepared to turn around if necessary. We strongly recommend that you update your mapping every year. This is best done online so that the satellite navigator's software can be updated at the same time; you may need help with this. Give yourself plenty of time as it takes a long time to download the mapping to the computer and then upload it to the navigator.

Some satellite navigators are pre-programmed with bridge heights and weight restrictions and we recommend that you confirm which countries are covered before purchasing. Having entered the dimensions and weight of your vehicle, the satellite navigator should avoid routes with bridges that are too low or roads with unsuitable weight and width restrictions. It is our opinion that this feature is unnecessary for motorhomes not exceeding 3m tall and less than 3,500kg. Garmin sells the Dezl as a large vehicle satellite navigator. Remember, it is essential that the satellite navigator takes all three types of coordinates.

Basic Kit

Motorhome manufacturers wishing to pass type approval follow the guideline in British Standard European Norm (BSEN) 1646-2 4.4 Personal Effects to ensure that enough weight is allocated for luggage, cooking and camping equipment.

The Standard provides manufacturers with the following weight calculation: 10x the number of berths, plus 10x the length in metres. This is easier to understand as 10kg per bed space and 10kg per linear metre. This equates to 110kg for a four berth, 7m motorhome and is supposed to be enough weight for four people's chattels. Our basic everyday equipment used by two people weighs 240kg. This is not surprising when you take into account shoes, bedding, food, drinks, kitchen, bathroom, and camping equipment, tools, oils, and vehicle-related liquid chemicals. Other items that are commonly carried but not included in our 240kg calculation might be bicycles, hobby equipment, laptop, camera, books, TV and satellite system. Each belted passenger seat has 75kg allocated (excluding driver). Therefore, a four-berth motorhome with three belted passenger seats has 225kg allowance for passenger weight. This is in addition to the Personal Effects allowance. Everyone is advised to weigh their loaded motorhome including the intended passengers, luggage and chattels, and full fuel and water tanks. See Chapter 2 to understand maximum weights and payload. In the unlikely event that you have any spare weight capacity you can consider adding the extras from your wish list. We strongly recommend that you make an inventory that includes the individual weights of each item carried.

Campernalia

Campernalia is an international multi-million pound industry providing a multitude of items for your every whim, from self-heating food to kitchen sinks. None of these are essential, but some are worth considering.

Awnings

Awnings can be used only at campsites or other areas where camping is permissible. If you predominantly intend to use Motorhome Stopovers or park offsite, then there is no point buying an awning. There are two types of awning that you can use at campsites. A wind-out awning is a fixed, roof-height roller blind that can be set up in a minute. This

Wind-out awnings should be used only where camping is permissible.

Free-standing awning.

provides useful shade, which also keeps the sun's heat off one side of the motorhome, and a dry area during light showers. Side panels are available for further comfort. This type of awning can be broken in windy conditions and awnings attached to the sides of motorhomes are easily damaged when driving in confined areas. A removable awning blind is the budget choice, but they take more effort to set up.

Free-standing awnings are ideal for campsite-based motorhomers pitching for a week or more at a time. This type of awning often resembles a tent and is self-supporting, so they can be left on pitch when the motorhome is taken offsite. In transit they are bulky, taking up valuable storage space and payload.

On The Level

Parking on level ground is an unusual luxury, whether at a campsite or at a Motorhome Stopover. When you are pitched at a campsite you can use levelling blocks, often referred to as chocks. The law forbids the use of levelling blocks when you are parking in a Motorhome Stopover or Offsite-Parking, so you will have to choose a parking area and

Bigger levelling blocks are required on this campsite pitch!

make do. Some motorhomes come with steadies; these are legs that can be wound to the ground to stop the motorhome rocking when stationary.

These are far from necessary and the effort of placing them down, and their weight, can negate their benefit. Once again, these must not be used at Motorhome Stopovers or when Offsite-Parking. Over time you will find that the motorhome is so rarely level that you begin not to notice.

Cab Window Screens

The cab windows provide very little thermal protection. Screens provide additional insulation in extremely hot or very cold weather. They also provide privacy if there are no curtains or interior concertina windscreen blinds. There are two types of temporary screen available, internal and external. External screens fit

Internal screens being used in a motorhome at a Motorhome Stopover at Dol de Bretagne, France.

over the outside of the motorhome, which means they can get wet and dirty and need to be dried and cleaned before storing. External screens should not be used when Offsite-Parking or at Motorhome Stopovers.

Internal screens are normally held in place with suckers on the glass.

Inevitably the screens touch the glass and become wet from condensation, therefore need to be dried before being stowed away. Another option is to retrofit Remis concertina blinds to the framework around the windows. Although expensive, they can be opened and closed in seconds and provide adequate insulation when closed.

External screens should not be used at Aires.

Mosquitoes are the one intruder that are guaranteed to join you in your motorhome. To keep them out every window and vent should be fitted with a secure fly-screen. This material is widely available and can be retrofitted if necessary. The door also needs protection and we found that a Fiamma Mosquito Net proved effective even in Finland where mosquitoes are prolific.

Air Conditioning/Cooling

Southern Europe is hot enough in August to justify the use of an air conditioning or cooling system, but for the majority of the time these are unnecessary. Before handing over a large amount of money, consider the power consumption and supply because most air conditioners require a 230V electricity supply and, even if they do not, they will drain your leisure battery quickly. Also consider the effects of the weight of the unit on the roof, the wind resistance, additional height, and the cost to run and service it. A cheap and simple alternative to air conditioning is a 12V fan fitted in a top vent. Fiamma and Omni Vent both produce models that work well. It is also worth fitting a top vent all weather cover. Top vent fans are sometimes standard equipment on new motorhomes and should be selected if on the options list. They can also be retrofitted, although wiring the 12V fan may prove challenging if there is no light close by to take a feed from. The fans fit into the common size top vents and can be switched to extract or blow air into the motorhome. Being reasonably quiet and as low as 0.5A, these are great as cooking/condensation extractors. When 230V is available you can use a fan or an oscillating fan heater with the heater elements turned off to create a breeze.

Additional Modes Of Transport

Motorhome Stopovers located in towns and villages tend to be within walking distance from shops, restaurants, and sites of interest. Campsites are usually located out of town and an additional mode of transport or public transport is usually required to get around.

Bicycles are the most practical and popular additional mode of transport used by motorhomers. Before you fit a bike rack, consider whether you will actually ride the bikes that have been collecting dust in your garage for years. Cycling is an excellent way of occupying yourself and keeping fit. Copenhagen and Stockholm are ideal cities to explore by bike and many other European towns

Bicycles are the most practical form of additional transport.

have bicycle routes. The best cycling countries are Belgium, Netherlands, Germany, Denmark and Hungary. Most national parks have cycle routes to explore and some have mountain bike routes. Spares and repairs are easy to get all over Europe and bikes are available to hire in many places. There are three types of bicycle to consider. If you only want to cycle gently to the shops or

Electric bicyles are practical transport.

around site, then a folding bike is perfect. If you want to make more of your bike, consider a hybrid bike that is a cross between a mountain and road bike; it should have at least ten gears. Couples with different cycling abilities could consider a tandem as the stronger cyclist will help the weaker and will not be constantly waiting. The Cycle Tourer website, www.cycletourer.co.uk, details cycling across Europe. Also worth checking are www.sustrans.org.uk/ncn/map/national-cycle-network and the European Cycling Federation, www.ecf.com.

Cycle racks are light and relatively unobtrusive, although bikes get dirty no matter how well you cover them. The Fiamma Carry Bike can hold up to 60kg; a standard bike weighs around 14kg, and an electric bike weighs 28kg (including the battery pack, but not the charger). Displaying a red and white striped hazard square to a rear protrusion is a legal requirement in

Another practical transport option? Perhaps it's a hobby trike.

some countries. These hazard signs are available from accessory shops at home and abroad. If your motorhome has a garage or large lockers consider storing your bikes inside. The motorhome's rear axle loading or available payload may dictate whether or not you can take bikes with you, see Chapter 2. Also ensure your travel insurance covers bicycle-related accidents.

Some motorhomes will not have sufficient weight capacities to carry a motorbike.

Scooters or motorbikes may seem like the ideal transport when the motorhome is parked on site. Unfortunately, few motorhomes, even those with garages, are legally capable of carrying the additional weight of a scooter once passengers and chattels are loaded, thus a trailer is necessary.

Scooters weigh about 100kg and a scooter rack weighs at least 70kg. See Chapter 2 to understand payload and rear axle loadings. We see more British-registered motorhomes towing cars than we do from all the other countries of Europe put together. We put this down to a lack of knowledge of Continental motorhome facilities. First-time Continental motorhome buyers will have seen motorhomes parked offsite and at official Motorhome Stopovers and may have a Motorhome Stopover in their town or village. In contrast, first-time UK buyers may not even know about Motorhome Stopovers or understand that it is normal not to stop at campsites. If you feel you need a car, we recommend that you buy a caravan as explained in Chapter 1.

There are two different ways to tow a car; the undisputed legal way is to load it onto a trailer and the other option is an A-frame system. The A-frame system is a convenient and simple solution once the car is adapted. A simple frame is attached to the front of the car which enables the car to be hitched to the motorhome like any other trailer. Although this system is not illegal in the UK, as long as trailer rules are complied with, this may bring unnecessary police attention to you in countries where it is unusual. Most people will not be able to reverse when an A-framed car is attached to the motorhome. In 2005 the Department of Transport released a fact

An A-frame towing system.

sheet entitled 'Note on A-Frames and Dollies' stating, '...we believe the use of "A" frames to tow cars behind other vehicles is legal provided the braking and lighting requirements are met. However, while this is our understanding of the meaning of the Regulations, it is only the Courts which can reach a definitive interpretation of the law.' People requiring further information should contact PRO-Tow Frames, manufacturers of CAR-A-TOW, www.caratow.com or Tel: 01202 632456.

Fitting a tow bar reduces the motorhome payload by at least 30kg. Licence holders restricted to towing 750kg will have to purchase a micro car or take a further driving test. Micro cars weighing less than 750kg MAM are built by Axiam (www.axiam.com), Microcar (www.microcar.co.uk), Ligier and DUÉ (www.leigier.fr).

This specialist trailer is available in France from www.labissonnette.fr.

Please remember that it is not reasonable to take up excessive space on a Motorhome Stopover because of your trailer, and some Motorhome Stopovers now ban trailers. Unhitching your trailer when Offsite-Parking or on a Motorhome Stopover is just the sort of thing that upsets local residents and causes restrictions to be applied. Campsites often charge extra for towed cars and trailers.

Entertainment

Television And Radio

Television is one of those things that seem to contradict the essence of motorhoming. Nevertheless, you will be glad of the entertainment on rainy days or long winter evenings. The digital switchover is complete in the UK and Europe, so make sure that your television and aerial are compatible. European countries sometimes broadcast programmes in English, often films, and you are likely to get the gist of the weather forecast in any language. Access to UK broadcast TV and radio is restricted as soon as you travel outside the intended range of reception. This subject is changing so quickly that we can generalise only.

Radios will work all over Europe as normal, except that you may not understand what the presenters are saying. The BBC's World Service is broadcast in Europe from a small number of local and national radio stations. You can see a frequencies list on the BBC's website, www.bbc.co.uk. The BBC World Service is also broadcast via satellite all over Europe Free-to-Air from Eutelsat Hot Bird 8 at 13° East, transponder 50, vertical polarisation, 11727 MHz, Service ID 13907. English digital feeds are also available from Eutelsat Hotbird13D, Astra 2E, Eutelsat 7A and Groupe Canal + in France. Do not worry if that made no sense because it is explained in satellite TV below.

Satellite dishes and receivers are relatively easy to set up and use, however the Astra 2 Ku Spot beam satellite signal, which broadcasts BBC, ITV, and many other channels, becomes weak outside of northern France and Benelux. According to users that have written to www.satelliteforcaravans.co.uk, it is possible to pick up the signal in the northern half of Spain, the Italian lakes and southern Germany. The ability to pick up the overspill signal depends upon dish size and good quality equipment. The Sky subscription service is broadcast over a bigger area and may be received half way down Spain and Italy. Users should read

Sky's terms and conditions before installing the satellite receiver in their motorhome. Freesat is another UK provider and Freesat receivers will display channels selected by that operator. Again the Astra 2 Ku Spot beam satellite is used. Free-to-Air compatible satellite receivers can lock into numerous satellites, as mentioned above, and receive signals from many European broadcasters. Buying a Free-to-Air receiver is a logical choice.

Satellite System Components:	
Satellite dish	Scart or HDMI lead
Coaxial	TV
Satellite decoder box	Tuner and compass

Televisions and satellite receivers that are powered by both 12V and 230V are preferable so that an inverter is not required. You can watch about ten hours of TV when you are relying on one 110Ah leisure battery, but then you will need to drive for several hours or hook-up to electricity to recharge the battery.

Most people fix the satellite dish to the motorhome roof, but trees and other obstructions are inevitable wherever you park and a few leaves is enough to block the signal. This is bad luck when you are Offsite-Parking, but campsite users may be able to chose a suitable pitch and can set up a free standing dish some way from their pitch as long as it does not cause inconvenience to others. Having chosen an area where you can aim the

Many European motorhomes have a folding satellite dish.

A satellite dish this big may pick up the UK broadcast in northern Spain.

satellite dish directly at the broadcasting satellite, use a compass and satellite finder to find the exact location. When setting up manually adjusted dishes, first adjust the elevation. Then adjust the LNB skew (polarisation) left or right. RoadPro has a PDF on their website under 'Tech Tips' that provides the angles. When searching for the Astra 2 Ku Spot beam, aim the dish to the east and adjust the satellite finder so it is not squeaking and no lights are on. Next turn the dish slowly to the right; it will pass over some weak signals. When it reaches 28.2 mil east on the military scale compass or 158° on a standard compass, depending on which you prefer to use, the finder will go off the scale. Turn the finder down to fine tune; fine tuning can also be done up and down if necessary. After a few seconds delay the signal strength and a lock indicator should come up on screen, this can take a while on the outskirts of the footprint. The principle is the same for all satellites except the angles will change. Bad weather weakens satellite signals and you may have to wait for it to pass before you can lock in to the satellite signal. Even once the satellite decoder is locked in, it may still lose signal during heavy rain or snow and strong wind may move the dish.

Surely you can watch TV and listen to radio online! Well, yes and no. All internet enabled devices are identified by an IP address when used on the internet. The IP address is normally generated by the internet service provider, and the address normally identifies the country that the device is being used in. UK TV and radio broadcasters are increasingly restricting access to UK IP addresses only. For example, if you use the WiFi at a Spanish campsite, the WiFi router will issue a Spanish IP address and many UK broadcasts will be unavailable.

Satellite internet systems work in much the same way as satellite TV. The satellite signal used is broadcast all over Europe, thus it may be possible to watch UK TV via the internet if the equipment installed in your motorhome has a UK IP address by default. See page 161 for further information.

RoadPro's motorhome has van-aerial disease despite frequent tests.

Satellite TV is an evolving medium, so please make further enquiries before purchasing a system. www.satelliteforcaravans.co.uk has detailed information on different types of satellite televisions, receiver boxes, and dish sizes for use in Europe. RoadPro sells satellite systems and provides detailed and useful information in their catalogue, visit www.roadpro.co.uk, Tel: 01327 312233.

Portable Computers

Portable computers can entertain you in so many ways and they are economical on 12V electricity. Modern laptops have vast memories and additional storage drives are inexpensive so you can store unlimited music, maps, tourist information, language courses, and audio and e-books. Also you can play games and watch films on DVDs or listen to CDs and they are also great for viewing and storing digital photos. If you dream of writing a book, now might be a good time to start. Try www.wordpress.com.

Consider securing your laptop in a laptop safe or by attaching a lock known as a Kensington lock. Laptops have a small hole that can accept a Kensington Lock and a wire hawser is looped around a secure object in the motorhome, such as a seat, making it hard for thieves to grab the laptop and run off.

Laptops can be secured with a Kensington lock.

Hobbies

Motorhoming is undoubtedly a hobby in its own right, but what are you going to do when you get there? We have observed that a typical day for Mr and Mrs Motorhomer involves just one hour away from the motorhome. The truth is motorhoming is boring

Campers enjoying a boules game.

unless you have something else to occupy your time. We recommend on the highest level that you plan your motorhoming tours around your hobbies and interests. Get a pen right now and write down all the things that you have ever wanted to do or see in Europe. Whittle them down, then research them thoroughly. Remember that poor planning produces poor results. Be sure you know which are the best places at different times of year and ensure you have the equipment you need with you. Bulky equipment may need special storage, such as a roof or bike rack-box. Beware these boxes can become the motorhome equivalent of a loft, and roof boxes create significant drag, so only fit when space is limited and spare payload is available. Arts and crafts make excellent motorhome hobbies as they are very time consuming and the equipment is often lightweight. Needlepoint, crochet, tapestry, and knitting are ideal and you may be able to sell your creations to other campers or present them to your friends and family upon your return. You are never short of something to draw, either from life or a postcard. Even if you have never drawn before, there are a range of books to get you started. Photography is an excellent hobby, not only can you record your travels, you could even sell your photos online. Search 'stock photos' for potential outlets and read the requirements. Why not share your experiences with your friends by uploading photos on social media sites, like Facebook or Pinterest, or onto your personal photo gallery or blog. Always consider security as you post.

Gather your walking information before you depart.

Our motto is: 'If in doubt, leave it behind'. That said, there have been days when we wanted to go swimming, walking or fishing and we did not know where to go, so make sure you have the relevant information with you.

Arabba Motorhome Stopover. Photo: Andy Glasgow.

Preparing Your Motorhome For A Winter Trip

First, remove all unnecessary items from the motorhome: summer chairs and tables, windbreaks, lanterns, flags, buckets and spades, BBQ, wetsuits, and summer clothes. Then load snow chains, a shovel, gloves, kneeling mat, water storage bottles (filled), hot water bottles, electric heater, hand brush, broom, cardboard/carpet, extra bedding, insulating screens, generator and fuel, tow rope/wire, winter clothes and shoes/boots. Now weigh your motorhome and see if there is any payload left for you, your luggage and food.

Ensuring your motorhome is in good working order is essential before embarking on a trip up the mountains. If you are in any doubt about the condition of your vehicle get it serviced or checked by a mechanic.

Tyres

Ensuring your vehicle has the correct tyres is the most important element of preparation if you want the best chance of staying on the road in icy conditions. Whilst preparing this guide we looked at the tyres fitted on a cross-section of UK motorhomes and campervans and discovered that 95 per cent were not fitted with winter tyres. Tyres with an M+S (mud and snow), snowflake, or snow-capped mountains image are winter-rated tyres. In our experience, Michelin M+S camper tyres perform extremely well in winter mountain conditions.

Winter tyre requirements vary from country to country. In Austria, winter-rated tyres or tyres marked M+S with a minimum tread depth of 4mm must be fitted from November to April. Snow chains are compulsory where signs indicate. Germany requires visitors to fit winter tyres and on-the-spot fines are issued to ill-prepared drivers that become stuck or impede the flow of traffic, so snow chains must be fitted when there is a covering of snow or ice. In France, snow chains must be fitted on vehicles driving on snow-covered roads when indicated by signs. In general, every country will expect winter visitors to be equipped to drive safely in snow, failure to do so could result in a fine.

Mountain routes may be impassable at any time between November and March. In northern Scandinavia, road closures due to snow are common until the end of May.

Go Motorhoming and Campervanning

Snow Chains

Snow chains fitted to the vehicle's driving wheels makes driving possible even in the iciest of conditions and it is advisable to carry snow chains in Andorra, Austria, France, Germany, Italy, and Switzerland. It is important to follow the Highway Code for each country and always follow chain manufacturer's instructions. Snow chains should only be fitted when the roads are completely covered in snow or ice.

Snow chains. Photos: Andy Glasgow.

Fitting snow chains for the first time is equivalent in difficulty to learning to ride a bike, so practice fitting and refitting them in warm, dry conditions until you can fit them without thinking about it. Wear tough but thin work gloves; thick leather gloves are useless when fitting fiddly chains. To assist in clearing snow around tyres it is worth carrying a stiff brush, a folding shovel, and a kneeling mat. Once fitted, drive 4-5m and then retighten the chains. When in use stop periodically to check the chains, and should you ever hear a repetitive clonking noise, stop immediately as a broken section of chain may be flailing around the inside of your wheel arch. Repair links are often supplied with chain sets for a temporary fix and, if necessary, a bungee will replace the elastic and can help to tighten the chains evenly. To prevent your chains from breaking: keep your speed down (in Germany the max speed is 50kph), and avoid harsh acceleration/braking, spinning wheels, and driving on asphalt. Also take care mounting levelling blocks and do not drive over the connectors when removing chains. Before you put the chains away rinse the salt off, then dry, untangle, and store between sheets of newspaper.

When making parking choices consider your exit and avoid parking down a slope. If snow is forecast, fit your chains before going out for the day or before bed.

Engine Condition And Fuel

Before embarking on a trip to the mountains it is important to ensure your vehicle is in good running order. Tired, older vehicles may struggle with the gradients, lower oxygen levels at altitude, and the cold. The vehicle's brakes should be checked to ensure they are in good condition before you undertake miles of steep descents.

In very cold conditions diesel solidifies into a waxy gel if antifreeze is not included. Depending when and where you buy diesel, you may also

Photo: Andy Glasgow.

need to buy and add special antifreeze to your fuel tank. For example, from early November all fuel stations in Austria change over to winter diesel rated to -20°C. However, if you buy fuel in southern Spain or Sicily, then climb into the mountains, park overnight, and wake up to -10°C or below, you won't be going anywhere until the diesel warms up. Diesel pumps at mountain fuel stations usually identify that the fuel is treated.

When outside temperatures fall and rise quickly, particularly overnight, atmospheric moisture condenses into water droplets on the inside of the fuel tank, above the fuel level. Truckers and farmers habitually fill up their fuel tanks at the end of the day to prevent this happening. Water is heavier than diesel and readily separates if the two are mixed together. Fuel filters catch water and slowly fill from the bottom up over time; this water can freeze and prevent fuel from reaching the engine. In freezing conditions you should regularly drain off the fuel filter. Simply unscrew the drain tap located at the bottom of the filter a couple of turns until diesel replaces water. You will need a receptacle to catch the water/diesel.

The only way you can be sure that there is enough antifreeze in your engine coolant system is to measure it with a hydrometer; these cost as little as £5. The ethylene glycol level needs to be between 40-50 per cent to withstand potential temperatures as low as -25°C. Also, ensure your screen wash is concentrated enough to cope with the cold. Check your vehicle handbook to confirm whether low-viscosity, cold-temperature oil is required for your engine. Your engine battery must also be in good condition, if in doubt take it to a garage to be tested.

Life In The Freezer – Preparing Your Utilities

Most modern motorhomes will be perfectly suitable for taking on a skiing holiday; although they are not known to be good skiers, they will provide warm and comfortable accommodation. The three utilities: gas, electricity and water need managing to ensure a comfortable trip. Make sure that your motorhome has recently had an annual habitation service and that the gas systems were serviced, not just visually inspected. Also, ensure that your carbon monoxide detector and smoke alarm are working.

What A Gas

Gas is essential for heating and cooking in your motorhome. Expect to consume one 11kg gas cylinder per week when not plugged into mains

Local gas cylinders available at fuel stations in France.

hook-up. Many people invest in refillable gas cylinders, but if you have two, leave one at home because you are going to have to use pure propane below 0°C and LPG Autogas across Europe nearly always includes some butane. Butane remains liquid below 0.5°C, but propane turns to gas as low as -42°C. In freezing temperatures the propane in your refillable cylinder is able to evaporate, leaving the butane as a liquid. Each time you fill up the percentage of butane in the cylinder increases. To get around this problem, use the refillable during warm days when the butane can evaporate and buy a local propane cylinder to use at night or when temperatures are below freezing. Remember to pack the appropriate pigtails.

Unfortunately, the simple gas convector heaters commonly fitted in caravans are rare in new motorhomes, apparently because of travel noise complaints. Their advantage over blown-air combi boilers is that they consume no 12V electricity in operation unless a supplementary blown-air system is used; an important point as 24-hour heating may be required whether the motorhome is occupied or not. If you are lucky enough to have a convector heater and it has a roof flue, ensure an extension pipe is fitted to prevent snow from burying the flue vent.

Go Motorhoming and Campervanning

Some campsites, for example in Austria, may offer metered mains propane gas. A flexible hose connects to your regulator and gas will be supplied at 50mbar, but your regulator will compensate if your system is set up for 30mbar. This may be a cost effective option if you plan to stop a long time.

Austrian mains gas. Photo: Andy Glasgow.

Electricity

Most new motorhomes will have a 12V, power-hungry, blown-air heating system. Using this unit will consume most of the available leisure battery supply; an 110Ah in good condition will provide power for 24 to 48 hours. It states in the Truma manual that a Combi 6 will use 5.6A at start up and 1.3A on average, but you will be using it in colder than average temperatures, thus it will use more than 1.3A. Solar panels will provide an insignificant amount of extra power and wind turbines could be a blowout. If you wish to visit a resort for more than 24 hours, the only reliable way to provide enough power is to plug into mains electricity or run a generator or fuel cell. There are plenty of open campsites and Motorhome

Electricity available from a pre-pay meter.

Stopovers around the ski resorts, many with electricity. The electric hook-up charge may be more than usual, but you will be using it all day and night to keep your motorhome warm and dry, so value for money is not an issue.

Campsites near ski slopes often have drying rooms and warm shower blocks. Small ski resorts may not have campsites, but Offsite-Parking may be tolerated in the gondola car park. When Offsite-Parking, a generator will be a necessity. Cheap 2-stroke generators are unpopular as the high pitched running noise and smelly fumes will soon annoy your neighbours. 4-stroke generators are quieter and very popular.

Photo: Andy Glasgow.

Water And Servicing

Visit a Service Point before ascending the mountains. It is common for water to be off or frozen at Motorhome Stopovers. Do not turn off water taps found running as the warmth in the water stops them freezing. Always fill up in the afternoon as taps are often frozen in the morning. Many people also carry drinking water in plastic containers inside the motorhome. Ensure you

Leave taps as you find them.

secure them in transit and check that they do not leak; this may be your only fresh water supply if your tank freezes.

Water and waste stored in under-slung tanks is prone to freezing. Insulation helps but the only way to ensure the water stays liquid is to fit a heater element. To prevent your water system and liquid goods from freezing you have to run heating constantly, possibly on the lowest setting during the day whilst you are out. If you run a blown-air system with ducts running through lockers, these should prevent any problems. Simple convector heaters, gas or electric, will not prevent pipes located in the depths of lockers from freezing. When researching *All the Aires Mountains*, the Glasgows found their water pump and drop valve suffered first, but keeping cupboard and internal locker doors open helped. Electric fan heaters can blow warm air into cold/damp spots and defrost frozen windscreens and other frozen areas like engines. Try to park so the sun warms up the side of the motorhome that contains the water pipes.

Most modern motorhomes have a built-in frost safety valve near the water heater. This valve opens automatically when the temperature gets close to freezing point; for example, Truma set their frost valve tripping point at 7°C. The opened valve then allows the water stored in the boiler to drain. If a pressure-sensing water pump is on, then all the water in the system will drain. This safety feature is very useful if you have laid up your motorhome for the winter, but not so useful if you are using it in cold conditions. The valve is unlikely to trip when the boiler is in use, but be aware that when using secondary electric heating (i.e. on electric hook-up) the water boiler cupboard will get cold. It states in the Truma manual that you can run the heater before you fill the boiler with water, thus bringing the temperature above 7°C. Additionally, a 0.4A heating element is available for the frost valve.

Keeping the waste water tank tap open and draining water into a container is good practice, but any residual waste water is still prone to freezing. Water expands by nine per cent when frozen, so do not fill your waste water tank completely and reduce the amount of water entering it. Use as many onsite facilities as possible and wash up in a bucket or bowl and dispose of the water at the onsite disposal point. The larger the amount of frozen water in your waste water tank, the longer it will take to defrost.

Before leaving your motorhome unused in cold weather, all liquids must be drained off (waste and fresh water and toilet waste) including all pipework as much as possible. Remember to drain your water heater, toilet flush, and sink drain traps, and remove the water filter. Open all drain valves and taps and then drive up and down steep hills to empty pipes. Leave the taps open with the hot/cold selector in the middle. Also remove all liquids and foods stored in cupboards that could spoil or burst if frozen.

Insulating Your Motorhome

Insulating screens are essential as the cab glass offers the least insulation of the whole caravan conversion. The cab itself offers the second least insulated area and curtains that isolate the cab area are worth retrofitting. We believe that, on balance, internal screens are preferable to externally fitted screens despite offering less

Photo: Andy Glasgow.

insulation. The condensation that forms on the windscreen often needs defrosting, then quickly removing with a squeegee. Van Comfort has a good range of screens, see www.vancomfort.co.uk.

Condensation occurs when airborne moisture condenses on a surface that is colder than room temperature. Removing your window screens in cold conditions demonstrates this instantly. The best way to control condensation is good ventilation, but this makes the occupants cold. Motorhomes are reasonably airtight apart

Use a squeegee to remove condensation.

from the intentional and essential vents, so do not block them with the exception of fitting the winter fridge covers. Vans converted to campervans can suffer draughts from the rear and sliding doors and may not have enough insulation.

Cooking and showering produce high levels of moisture. Gas releases one litre of water for every litre burnt, so avoid long cooking sessions. Always cook with lids on pans, keep a top vent open, run extractors if fitted, and turn the heating up to compensate as this also helps to expel the steam. Keep up the regime whilst eating and until the washing up is dried. Shower with the top vent ajar, use blown-air heating if available and squeegee the walls dry as soon as possible. Use the bathroom as your airing cupboard for damp clothes and towels and keep the top vent ajar and heating vent open. Fan heaters help to keep the air moving, thus preventing some condensation build-up. When driving between sites run the cab heating fans on full. Should you be lucky enough to get too hot, open a rear window or top vent to create a through draught.

In really cold weather you may need to insulate every window. All you need is bubble wrap, double-sided sticky tape, scissors, and some attachable suction pads. These items are available from most DIY stores in Europe. Simply tape two or more layers of bubble wrap together and cut to the right size for your window. Windows with roller blinds will hold the bubble wrap in place. Use suction pads to hold the bubble wrap in place on cab windows. We have tested these home-made screens down to -18°C and found they helped considerably.

A second layer of carpet, or plastic runner, on the floor offers extra insulation, takes the wear and tear, and can be discarded at the end of the season. We also lay cardboard above the carpet to absorb the inevitable water that comes in each time you enter the motorhome. We recommend you lay cardboard before border posts to protect the carpet from the wet, and often muddy, boots of the customs officials.

Bedding

Andy Glasgow loves sleeping in his Luton.

To keep warm in the cold we use a four-duvet system in winter; it sounds over the top, but it works well. Typical 5" foam mattresses or cushions do not offer enough comfort or insulation, so one covered duvet is used as a mattress topper/sheet and all duvets are laid on the bed. Then, depending on how cold it is, you can choose to sleep under one, two or three duvets. Place hot water bottles in beds one hour before retiring. Choose bottles with thick fluffy covers as they stay warm all night. Hooded tops are ideal for sleeping in when it is really cold. Andy and Sue Glasgow, who researched *All the Aires Mountains* by Vicarious Books, love their Luton over-cab bed as they find it the warmest place to be. The top tip is Do not let yourself get cold before going to bed because it takes ages to warm up and stops you from sleeping.

Poor bladder control may not be the culprit of bed wetting in very cold conditions. Moisture constantly evaporates from our skin and beds suffer a build up during prolonged use. When the base of the bed is cold, moisture naturally condenses where the mattress touches it. This is a real problem on beds without slats, but an underlay mat helps to keep the air moving, www.shipshapecaravans.co.uk. Make a conscious effort to air the mattress or cushions daily; simply propping them up should be enough.

Froli bed systems improve comfort and ventilation. www.novaleisure.com.

Snow On The Roof

The title is not intended as a euphemism, more a warning. Snow is known as a good insulator, but thawing and refreezing could create your very own rooftop glacier. Sweep off fresh snow as soon and as best as you can. Pressure washers may help remove ice on roofs.

Photo: Andy Glasgow.

Take great care on the roof of your motorhome in winter – it's like an ice skating rink. Ensure a build up of snow does not block vents and flues. This is a daily task and it is good practice to sweep the area around the motorhome as well to keep it clear, dry and ice free. There is nothing more frustrating than injuring yourself by falling over in the parking area.

A shovel is essential to dig your motorhome out of the snow, this sounds fun but a few days of freezing temperatures, high winds and blizzards will shorten the fuse of any camper.

Andy Glasgow clears snow from the roof. Photo: Sue Glasgow.

Winter fridge vents fitted. Photo: Andy Glasgow.

Storing Your Equipment

Whatever your chosen mountain pursuit, it is likely to involve some wet, muddy clothes and some cumbersome or sharp equipment. Most people opt to dry clothes in the shower cubicle, but you need to think about how you are going to hang them up. Boxes lined with newspaper are ideal for muddy boots. Skis have very sharp edges which

Store your equipment carefully. Photo: Andy Glasgow.

can easily mark fixtures and fittings, so you need to consider how you are going to store them. Some people attach their skis to their rear ladder, but if you leave any of your equipment outside you must make sure it is under lock and key.

Life On The Road

Once you are on the road it is important that you travel safely and carry out regular maintenance to stop issues becoming problems. Even summer travellers should consider that temperatures are lower up mountains. Mountain resorts can be isolated with limited supplies. Out of season (spring and autumn), shops may be closed. Before arriving at your chosen resort, stop in the lower valleys to stock up with anything you may need. Fill up the water tank and extra water bottles if you carry them. Empty the toilet and the waste water tank. Check the gas levels and fill up or exchange if necessary. Stock up with food, but remember that some packet food will expand as you increase altitude so make sure it has enough space.

Driving Mountain Roads

Mountain roads are often narrow and twisty and it takes both skill and concentration to safely drive them. General etiquette dictates that on narrow mountain lanes the driver heading downhill is expected to pull over when traffic is met coming uphill. Driving with dipped headlights or daylight running lights significantly reduces the risk of head-on collision. Sounding the horn on twisting roads with reduced visibility is highly recommended. Study maps and plan routes carefully as difficult or dangerous sections of roads are often marked and are best avoided. In

Mountain roads are often narrow and twisty.

winter and spring, high passes may be closed due to snow, snow drifts or wind. Never drive down a route marked as closed or open closed gates.

Driving down a mountain with a fully loaded motorhome takes a lot more skill than in a car, especially in snow. You have to descend slowly and utilise your gears, only using the brakes when necessary. Brake fade is the name given to loss of braking due to overheating. When brakes overheat this heat alters the characteristics of the compounds resulting in friction being lost and therefore reduced braking and induced fear. The warning signs are a strong chemical smell similar to burning electrics or metal being cut by an angle-grinder. Pulling over and allowing brakes to cool should make them function again, but if they have reached the stage of smoke coming from the wheels it may be too late. If you have suffered brake fade and have any doubt on their condition, get them checked by a qualified engineer.

Avoidance is always the best strategy, so descend in the same gear you used to ascend; if third gear is too fast, instead of braking change down to second gear. Do not rest your foot on the pedal, just brake harder periodically.

Never drive a mountain route signed as closed.

When descending on snow and/or ice remember that the brakes apply to all wheels whereas engine braking applies only to the engine-driven wheels (i.e. front-wheel-drive). Therefore, if you suddenly drop down a gear you may cause a loss of traction. Traction may also be lost if you apply harsh braking, so be gentle. Don't worry about the local traffic. However fast you drive it will not be fast enough for them, so pull over where you can and let them past. Avoid departing from the ski resort exactly as the lifts close or arriving just before the lifts open as you will be battling locals who won't appreciate you being there. Aim to drive during the day in clear weather. Always check the weather forecasts before departing and call in at local tourist offices to check the routes and resorts are open. Where possible, avoid driving at night or during falling snow, high winds or fog.

Out And About

Winter visitors should have the latest edition of *Where to Ski and Snowboard* (www.wheretoskiandsnowboard.com) so they can assess the resorts. There are several walking guidebooks by Cicerone, Lonely Planet, and Sunflower Books which cover short and long walks. Tourist guides, such as the French Alps guide by Michelin, provide information on tourist sites as well as some walks and drives.

Before engaging in any mountain pursuits make sure you do your homework. Ensure you have the correct insurance just in case mountain rescue is required. Ski insurance can be purchased with lift passes for €1-€2, however good travel insurance is always recommended. Before heading out for the day, check weather reports and pack clothes for all weather as it can change quickly in the mountains. Also, it's important not to overestimate your ability and build in extra time as a contingency for whatever activity you plan. When setting out on a journey, carry as much information as possible to navigate with. Ensure you have maps and a compass and do not rely solely on pre-placed footpath markers. When possible, let someone know where you are going and what time you will return.

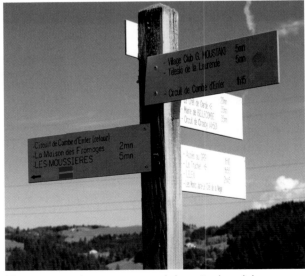

Use maps and a compass and do not rely solely on pre-placed footpath markers.

CHAPTER 5 – Documentation

Knowing that everybody loves paperwork, we have made this chapter as vibrant as possible. Read this chapter carefully so that you understand the implications of what you are doing and what documentation you are legally required to travel with.

Passports And Identification

Your passport is the most important document that you travel with and may be the only documentation recognised as personal identification. Before you book your crossing, check that everybody travelling with you has an undamaged and valid passport that has an expiration date no less than six months after your intended return date. The following countries require you to carry your passport at all times as identification: Bulgaria, Cyprus, Czech Republic, Estonia, the Netherlands, Slovakia, Bosnia and Herzegovina, Croatia, Montenegro and Serbia. When you are not required to carry your passport keep it in a secure place, preferably a safe, and avoid handing it over to anyone unless necessary. If you need to renew your British passport or have any passport related questions, visit www.gov.uk/browse/abroad/passports.

The Camping Card International (CCI) is a credit card-sized card that displays the holder's name, address, and passport number. The CCI is worth buying because campsite receptionists will accept them as alternatives to your passports which are normally asked for when booking in and are often kept then overnight. Each CCI has 2,500,000 Swiss Francs worth of third-party insurance against accidental damage at campsites. Discounts are offered to holders at 2,500 campsites, visit www.campingcardinternational.com. CCI cards cost from £5.50 and are available from organisations affiliated to the AIT, FIA or FICC. Members can buy CCI from: The Motor Caravanners' Club, The Camping & Caravanning Club, Hymer Club International, and RAC. AA personal members may purchase a CCI from The Camping & Caravanning Club quoting their AA membership number. Have the following information on hand when you phone: date and place of birth, nationality, passport number, passport date and place of issue.

Camping Key Europe cards will be required if touring Scandinavia. See www.campingkey.com.

Warning: enhanced interior security.

Pet Passports

The Pet Travel Scheme (PETS) allows you to take your domestic dogs and cats, or ferrets to many European countries without quarantine. If you wish to travel with a different species contact the Department for Environment, Food and Rural Affairs (DEFRA), www.defra.gov.uk, Tel: 0207 2386951.

PETS requirements and limitations as of February 2015:

- Restricted to domestic dogs and cats, and ferrets.
- First, your pet must be microchipped with an ISO standard microchip.
- Next, the animal must undergo a course of rabies vaccinations (21-day movement restriction applies).
- Then obtain an EU pet passport from an official veterinarian or from your local Animal Health and Veterinary Laboratories Office.
- Passports are designed to last the life of the animal. They confirm the microchip number, the date of implant, and the rabies vaccination record.
- Rabies vaccinations are valid for three years, to re-validate the passport a booster vaccination is needed before the expiration date of the previous vaccination.
- Only five pets per owner are allowed in transit at any one time (exceptions apply).
- Dogs must have tapeworm treatment before entering the UK, see below.

The PETS scheme allows your pet to travel with you without restriction to the following EU countries: Austria, Belgium, Bulgaria, Croatia, Cyprus, Czech Republic, Denmark, Estonia, Finland, France, Germany, Gibraltar, Greece, Greenland, Hungary, Ireland (UK-based pets do not need a passport to enter Ireland and vice versa), Italy, Latvia, Lithuania, Luxembourg, the Netherlands, Poland, Portugal, Romania, Slovakia, Slovenia, Spain, Sweden and the UK. Non-EU European countries included in the PETS scheme are: Andorra, Belarus, Bosnia and Herzegovina, Faroe Islands, Iceland, Liechtenstein, Norway, the Russian Federation, and Switzerland. Worldwide countries include Australia, New Zealand, Canada and the United States (mainland).

Before travelling, visit www.defra.gov.uk/wildlife-pets/pets/travel/ for up-to-date information. Some countries require additional forms and many countries require an Export Health Certificate and/or an import licence.

Not all ferries accept pets and special requirements and additional costs may apply. www.defra.gov.uk provides information about approved rail and ferry routes that allow pets to travel to and from the UK under the PETS scheme. Also check that your pet insurance covers your pet in Europe. For any queries about PETS contact pettravel@ahvla.gsi.gov.uk, Tel: 037 0241 1710. Further information can also be found on the EU website http://europa.eu/travel/pets.

Under the Pet Travel Scheme, dogs entering the UK must be treated for Echinococcus multilocularis tapeworm no less than 24 hours and not more than 120 hours (1-5 days) before they are scheduled to arrive. Dogs entering the UK directly from Finland, Ireland, Malta or Norway are exempt from treatment. A qualified vet must carry out the treatment and record it in the pet passport. The record must include the practice stamp and vet's signature, the date and time administered, and the name of the product and manufacturer, which must contain Praziquantel. www.passportforpets.co.uk provides details of suitable vets near ports; click on the red crosses on the map for vet names and phone numbers.

Don't tread on the cat's stool!

The white cliffs of Dover.

Escaping The UK

Unless you have an amphibious motorhome, you will have to pay to get to mainland Europe and that can be very expensive at peak times during August bank holiday weekends. Money can be saved all year by travelling off peak. Typically mornings are peak when departing the UK and evenings are peak for return. Booking directly online is normally cheapest. Tesco Clubcard points are worth three to one at Eurotunnel. Purchasing Frequent Traveller tickets may prove cost effective even without using all of the tickets. We have found that the savings made against return crossings in August covered most of the initial cost. Frequent Traveller perks include boarding the next available crossing regardless of booking; although peak supplements may apply.

Sometimes it is quicker, or cheaper, to use ferries instead of roads, so consider your options. Some overnight ferries can only be booked with a cabin, but others will allow you to camp on board in your motorhome so ask before you book a cabin. Unfortunately, there are no ferries departing or arriving in the UK that allow camping on board.

Company	Ports and crossings	Contact details
Brittany Ferries	Portsmouth – Caen, Cherbourg, Le Havre, and St Malo (France); Santander and Bilbao (Spain). Poole – Cherbourg (France). Plymouth – Roscoff and St Malo (France); Santander (Spain). Cork – Roscoff (France).	www.brittany-ferries.co.uk Tel: 0871 2440744
DFDS	Dover – Dunkerque and Calais (France). Newcastle – Amsterdam and IJmuiden (the Netherlands). Newhaven – Dieppe (France).	www.dfdsseaways.co.uk Tel: 0871 5747235
Euro Tunnel	Folkestone – Calais (France).	www.eurotunnel.com Tel: 0844 3353535
P&O Ferries	Dover – Calais (France). Hull – Rotterdam (the Netherlands); Zeebrugge (Belgium). Liverpool – Dublin. Larne – Troon and Cairnryan.	www.poferries.com Tel: 08716 646464
MyFerryLink	Dover – Calais (France).	www.myferrylink.com Tel: 0844 2482100
Stena Line	Belfast – Cairnryan and Liverpool. Dublin and Dun Laoghaire – Holyhead. Harwich – Hook Van Holland (the Netherlands). Rosslare – Cherbourg (France); Fishguard.	www.stenaline.co.uk Tel: 0844 7707070

A Brittany Ferries cabin.

Channel Tunnel, Folkestone.

Ferry journeys cannot be compared to cruising and we have developed a ferry survival strategy for any crossing where we are obliged to leave the motorhome. On short crossings, we take a flask of tea. If the journey coincides with a mealtime, we either eat at an onboard restaurant or bring food with us. We always carry our laptop onboard so that we can watch a DVD and listen to it on headphones. We also pack the laptop charger and Continental plug adaptor as it is often possible to sit near a plug socket. On longer journeys with a cabin we take the same kit, but include more DVDs and take our electric kettle, teabags, UHT milk and five litres of drinking water. Motorhome gas cylinders must be turned off during ferry journeys, but on longer crossings it may be possible to plug the motorhome into an electric point so that the fridge can run. Sometimes the plug sockets are located in the deck roof and staff lower them with a pole, on other ferries they are on the walls. Sometimes electric cables crossing the deck are stuck down with adhesive tape for safety reasons.

Avoid the fjords area of Norway if you are not keen on ferries as the roads frequently end abruptly and a ferry has to be taken to continue the journey. The ferry embarkation experience is normally confusing, but never more frantic than in Greece where you may be asked to reverse on or off a ferry. Beware of grounding when entering or exiting the ferry and watch out for other motorists or pedestrians. Out of season, timetables at small ports should be treated more as guidance than fact. Tickets for long crossings can be purchased from brokers near the ports or on board for short trips. Ferries can be delayed or cancelled due to weather or other unforeseen circumstances, so try and avoid pre booking ongoing travel arrangements that do not allow for delays.

Travelling Within The European Union

EU citizens and citizens from Norway, Iceland and Switzerland can travel and stay in another EU country for up to three months without a visa, providing they have a valid passport. This includes: Austria, Belgium, Bulgaria, Croatia, Cyprus, Czech Republic, Denmark, Estonia, Finland, France, Germany, Greece, Hungary, Ireland, Italy, Latvia, Lithuania, Luxembourg, Malta, the Netherlands, Poland, Portugal, Romania, Slovakia, Slovenia, Spain, Sweden, and the UK. The same freedom applies in the following countries in the European Economic Area (EEA): Norway, Iceland, and Liechtenstein; and Switzerland allows the free movement of goods and people. EU citizens also have the right to reside in another EU country. If you plan on staying more than three months, you are obliged to register

Some borders in Europe are little more than a sign due to the Schengen Agreement.

residency with that country. However, failing to register does not remove the right to reside in that country. This legislation is of little consequence to EU citizens travelling around Europe unless they intend to reside permanently in another country.

Since 1995, travellers have been enjoying an increasingly borderless Europe thanks to the Schengen Agreement. There are border controls when entering and exiting the Schengen area, but once inside the area people are allowed to travel between member countries without the inconvenience of border checks. Currently, 25 countries form the Schengen zone: Austria, Belgium, Czech Republic, Denmark, Estonia, Finland, France, Germany, Greece, Hungary, Iceland, Italy, Latvia, Lithuania, Luxembourg, Malta, the Netherlands, Norway, Poland, Portugal, Slovakia, Slovenia, Spain, Sweden, and Switzerland.

The Schengen system was absorbed into EU law in 1999 within the Amsterdam Treaty. Despite this, the UK and Ireland are exempt from adopting the Schengen system. Although the Schengen area does not have internal borders, officials have the right to ask you to identify yourself by showing your passport or ID card. Be aware that driving licences, post, bank, or tax cards may not be accepted as identification. Countries can reinstate borders should they wish to, but this is unusual.

Australian, Canadian, New Zealand, and USA passport holders without criminal records do not need to apply for a Schengen visa for visits of less than 90 days. Although a physical visa is not required, passport checks will be recording your movements in and out of the Schengen area. This has the same effect as if you had category C Schengen visa, which limits non-EU citizens to a maximum of 90 days over a 180-day period from the date of entry into the Schengen area. You can come and go as you please during the 180-day period as long as you do not exceed 90 days within the

Schengen area. Once the first 180-day period has elapsed, you can start again. Exceeding 90 days is treated as illegal residency and being caught could result in a fine, deportation, registration as an offender on the Schengen Information System (SIS) and possibly a criminal record.

Observant readers will have noted above that the UK and Ireland are not part of the Schengen area despite being in the EU. Australian, New Zealand, United States and Canadian tourists can visit the UK for up to six months visa-free and be out of the Schengen area. You can also visit Albania, Belarus, Bosnia and Herzegovina, the former Yugoslav Republic of Macedonia, Moldova, Montenegro, Russia, Serbia and the Ukraine or maybe include a trip to Morocco. Remember to obtain the necessary visas to visit these countries and to get your passport stamped every time you enter or exit the Schengen area to ensure you can prove you have not outstayed your welcome.

Visa requirements are complicated and subject to changes and conditions. Always check you have current information by contacting the relevant embassies before you travel. Further information on the Schengen agreement and travelling within the European Union can be found at http://ec.europa.eu/dgs/home-affairs/what-we-do/policies/borders-and-visas.

Travelling Outside The European Union

British passport holders travelling outside the EU will need to check entry requirements and read the advice given at the foreign office website www.gov.uk/foreign-travel-advice. Ensure you get your passport stamped on entry and exit.

At the time of publication, 90-day tourist visas were automatically given to British passport holders upon entry into the following countries: Albania, Andorra, Armenia, Bosnia and Herzegovina, Georgia, Iceland, Kosovo (although visitors may need to prove why they are visiting), Liechtenstein, Macedonia, Moldova, Montenegro, Morocco, Norway, Serbia, Switzerland, Tunisia and Ukraine.

Azerbaijan, the Russian Federation, and Turkey all require British passport holders to obtain visas. Visas may need to be applied for in advance so confirm this before you leave home. Ensure that your passport is valid for six months after your entry and that you obtain a stamp in your passport at the point of entry and exit.

British passport holders require a visa to visit Australia. Applications can be made online for free at www.immi.gov.au/visitors/tourist/evisitor and notification of the visa result is sent to you via email. If you are over 75 you may need to undergo a health check for your tourist visa, visit www.immi.gov.au/allforms/health-requirements. British passport holders visiting New Zealand for less than six months do not need a visa providing an onward ticket has been booked and the passport is valid for at least one month from the date of exit.

British passport holders can visit the United States for 90 days without a visa through the Visa Waiver Programme (VWP). Visitors must register with the VWP website in advance of their trip at https://esta.cbp.dhs.gov and pay an administration charge of around $14. You will then be notified if you can visit the United States without a visa. Once accepted, the visa waiver is valid for two years or until your passport expires, whichever comes first, but no single stay may exceed 90 days. British passport holders can visit Canada without a visa, but ensure you have at least six months validity on your passport after your intended return. You may also need to prove that you can financially support yourself throughout your stay, even if you are staying with friends and family.

Non-British passport holders need to check their entry requirements before visiting the above countries. Visa information is usually provided by your government. Australian passport holders should visit http://smartraveller.gov.au, New Zealand passport holders should visit www.safetravel.govt.nz, United States passport holders should visit http://travel.state.gov, and Canadian passport holders should visit www.voyage.gc.ca.

If you are travelling to or from any country not discussed above, check with the relevant embassy or at www.gov.uk/foreign-travel-advice for entry requirements and further information.

Driving Licences

Anyone intending to drive abroad must have their full valid driving licence with them. Provisional, expired or disqualified driving licences do not entitle the holder to drive abroad. Driving licences issued in the EU allow an EU citizen to drive anywhere in the EU in any vehicle the holder is entitled to drive.

UK driving licence, front. Image: DVLA.

UK driving licence, rear. Image: DVLA.

Photo-card only licences are issued in most countries and people with a pre 1989 paper driving licence may need to show their passport as photo identification. It is recommended that UK paper licences be surrendered to the DVLA for replacement with a photo licence; alternatively buy an International Driving Permit. The abolition of the paper counterpart licence in June 2015 voids all in existence. Points and penalties will be recorded digitally. Photo licences are valid for 10 years from the date of issue, the date of renewal is marked on the licence so check now.

Driving licences detail the vehicle categories each holder is entitled to drive and any restrictions and penalties. Your licence may be requested at a roadside check, if stopped for a traffic violation, involved in an accident, or by vehicle hire staff. If you passed your driving test in the UK before 1st January 1997, unless other restrictions apply, your licence will include category C1 with restriction 107 applied. This allows you to drive a vehicle with a MAM weight of 7,500kg and a GTW weight up to 8,250kg if towing a trailer. Drivers reaching the age of 70 will lose any entitlement to drive vehicles over 3,500kg unless a medical is passed and a Medical Examination Report is submitted to the DVLA.

If you passed your driving test after 1st January 1997, you have a category B licence and are entitled to drive a vehicle with a MAM of 3,500kg plus a 750kg trailer. Braked trailers over 750kg may be towed if the combined MAMs of the vehicle and trailer do not exceed 3,500kg, but the trailer MAM must be less than the tow vehicle unladen weight. If you wish to drive a vehicle heavier than 3,500kg you need to take a C1 driving test. Further information regarding driving licences and online forms are available from www.gov.uk/browse/driving, or pick up a form from the Post Office.

International Driving Permits (IDP) are not needed in the EU if you have a

British photo driving licence. A current list of countries that require an International Driving Permit is available on the application form and suppliers' websites. At the time of publishing, the list contained the following European countries: Albania, Belarus, Bosnia and Herzegovina, Bulgaria, Croatia, Czech Republic, Georgia, Iceland, Kazakhstan, Macedonia, Montenegro, Romania, the Russian Federation, Serbia, Turkey and Ukraine. British driving licence holders are advised to carry an International Driving Permit if driving in Australia, Canada, Morocco, Tunisia and the United States.

The International Driving Permit displays a photo of the driver and the text is printed in several languages. They can only be issued to valid driving licence holders over the age of 18 and are valid for 12 months. You can purchase one from the AA (www.theaa.com) or the RAC (www.rac.co.uk) and the Post Office (www.postoffice.co.uk). Non-EU driving licence holders are recommended to obtain an IDP from their automotive association before they travel to Europe. Even if you travel with an IDP you will still need to take your current driving licence with you.

Vehicle Requirements

Automotive and traffic law is not completely harmonised across the EU, but a vehicle compliant with the laws of the registered country is usually accepted in another EU country for up to six months. This means your UK-registered road vehicles must have valid road tax, insurance and MOT. If you intend to keep a vehicle in a single EU country longer than six months, visit http://europa.eu/youreurope/citizens/vehicles/registration/index_en.htm for further information.

MOT

UK legislation requires privately used motorhomes over three years old to pass an annual class IV (4) environmental and road safety inspection, known in the UK as an MOT. An MOT must be carried out at a registered Department of Transport testing station. The initial three year period when an MOT is not required is calculated from the date of first registration with the DVLA. Vehicles can be MOT'd at any time whether or not the current MOT has expired. A vehicle can be MOT'd up to 31 days in advance so the new one starts as the existing one expires, therefore 13 months' MOT is possible. If you intend to carry goods for commercial activity and your motorhome weighs between 3,000kg and 3,500kg, it needs to pass a class

MOT testing bay at Eric Road Test Centre, Dover.

VII (7) MOT. If your motorhome weighs over 3,500kg, it needs to be tested as a goods vehicle. There has been some confusion amongst the motorhome community whether or not such things as scooters used for pleasure are deemed as goods. The Vehicle and Operator Services Agency (VOSA), who oversee MOT testing, provided us with the following statement: *'In our view anything that the driver and his friends or family might reasonably be taking to use recreationally on their trip would be fine. Anything that they are taking either to sell or to use in any commercial activity may not be, depending on the particular circumstances... As far as we are aware there have been no cases of the Police treating [recreational] items as goods when carried on a motorhome.'*

There are no approved MOT testing stations outside of the UK and equivalent foreign tests, including tests in British overseas territories such as Gibraltar, are not accepted. If you are planning to be away when your vehicle either requires its first or annual MOT inspection, you have no choice but to bring it back to the UK. Eric Road Test Centre in Dover has an MOT bay that is suitable for motorhomes up to 5,000kg and no taller than 3.63m (11'11"). Both class IV and VII tests can be taken. You can book an MOT test online at www.motdover.co.uk or by phone on (0044) 01304 242233. Eric Road Test Centre, Eric Road, Dover, CT17 0TE, N51°08.133' E001°17.835'.

Road Fund Licence

Paper tax discs are no longer issued, however every UK road-registered vehicle must be registered for vehicle tax when used on the public highway, including Europe, even if it is tax exempt. Tax can be purchased for periods of either six or twelve months and can be purchased two months in advance. The vehicle must have a valid MOT. Renewing the tax online is easy because the DVLA website instantly checks that the vehicle is eligible. Concessionary rates apply. All vehicle tax information is available at the Post Office and at www.gov.uk.

Having UK road tax does not exempt you from paying road tolls in Europe. Usually tolls are chargeable on motorways and on some bridges. The AA website (www.theaa.com) provides toll road information. Countries, such as Austria, which have a one-off charge are detailed in the country guides at www.go-motorhoming.co.uk. Be aware that maximum time limits apply on some toll roads and these limits should be shown on the ticket. For example, France is limited to 24 hours and Portugal to 12 hours. Failing to exit in time may result in additional charges. We strongly advise against spending the night at a motorway service station because of the risk of burglary and the possibility of exceeding time restrictions.

Chris paying a French toll by credit card.

Low emission zones, congestion charges, and exclusion zones are now common in large European cities. Each country has its own rules and regulations, thus specific country and city research is necessary. www.lowemissionzones.eu details the low emission zones within the EU and further details are provided on www.go-motorhoming.co.uk.

Check your toll ticket: This one for the A1 in Portugal clearly identifies that you must complete your journey within 12 hours.

Insurance

There are plenty of insurance companies and policies to choose from, and even more variations in the level of cover provided. Your first choice is whether or not you want comprehensive insurance that covers the cost of repairs if the motorhome is accidently damaged, or provides compensation should your motorhome be written-off or stolen. Most people buy insurance that provides comprehensive cover in the UK and Europe, but check that the Europe cover is not reduced to third party, fire and theft. Some policies restrict European travel to as little as 30 days per year, although most now offer 180 days. Some policies that state they offer 365 days European cover do not allow this to be taken continuously. Some insurance policies are designed for cars, so check whether specialist items such as awnings are insured and that the value of contents insurance is sufficient; realistically this needs to be at least £3,000. Some insurance policies have age restrictions for drivers under 30 or over 75 years old or do not insure vehicles over 25 years old. Always check the small print and make sure the following are included in the policy:

- The motorhome will be repatriated (brought home) if you become incapable of driving it, or it is not roadworthy following an accident.
- A 24-hour, 365-days-a-year English language helpline is available.
- An alternative motorhome or accommodation is offered in the event of an accident or loss.
- A bail bond is offered should the vehicle be impounded after an accident in Spain.

Also confirm the following:

- Territorial limits. What countries are covered and what level of cover is there for each? Usually all EU countries will be offered at the same level of cover. Check whether European cover is comprehensive and check how you get Green Cards for additional countries.
- What factors invalidate your insurance? Travelling without current road fund licence, MOT or exceeding the vehicle weight limits will probably invalidate your insurance.
- Check for annual mileage restrictions.
- If vehicle recovery is included, what happens if the motorhome breaks down? Are roadside repairs undertaken or are you simply recovered to the nearest garage?

Some insurance brokers offer motorhome-specific policies. Comfort Insurance offers a policy with 365 days continuous travel. This policy is suitable for people living in their motorhome full-time in the UK and/or Europe who may have no fixed address, visit www.comfort-insurance.co.uk, Tel: 0800 0304206. The Camping and Caravanning Club can offer 365 days continuous EU cover to members up to the age of 80 as long as it is requested when taking out the policy. Saga specialises in insurance for the over 50s and has no upper age limit. They also automatically offer unlimited EU cover when you take your motorhome abroad, visit www.saga.co.uk, Tel: 0800 0964553. Adrian Flux specialises in providing insurance for the unusual and old, such as classic VW campervans, self-build and unusual conversions, RVs, and high-end European motorhomes, visit www.adrianflux.co.uk, Tel: 0800 3698590. DownUnder Insurance Services provides insurance for British-registered vehicles owned by Australians, Americans, Canadians, New Zealanders and South Africans over 20 years old and Brits over 25. Policies allow up to 12 months' travel in the UK and Europe in vehicles less than 32 years old, free from major modifications, and with no more than seven seats. Up to four named drivers can be registered on the policy, visit www.duinsure.com, Tel: 0800 393908. Day Insure provide short-term cover, 28 days or less, for UK-registered vehicles, visit www.dayinsure.com, Tel: 0845 4506615.

The following insurance providers also offer motorhome-specific insurance policies: The Caravan Club, www.caravanclub.co.uk, Tel: 01342 336633, Safeguard, www.safeguarduk.co.uk, Tel: 0800 9775953, Caravan Guard www.caravanguard.co.uk, Tel: 0800 1488400, and Campton, www.campton.co.uk, Tel: 01883 742460.

Insurance policies issued within the EU must provide the minimum insurance cover required by law in every EU country, which is third-party cover. Comprehensive policies will exceed that requirement. Your motorhome Certificate of Motor Insurance lists the countries covered within the territorial limits. Should you wish to travel to a country not in the territorial limits you will need to purchase an International Motor Insurance Card, known as a Green Card. A Green Card proves that you have the minimum legal requirements for third-party liability insurance required by law in a specific country. The Green Card system operates in Europe and countries bordering the Mediterranean. Green Cards are required in Albania, Belarus, Bosnia and Herzegovina, the former Yugoslav Republic of Macedonia, Montenegro, Morocco, Russia, Serbia, Tunisia, Turkey and

Ukraine. Green Cards can often be purchased from your insurance provider in advance or local insurance can be purchased at the border of the country. It is worth noting that your insurance provider may not provide you with an actual green card when they send you your insurance documents, some simply print an explanation on the reverse of your Certificate of Motor Insurance in multiple languages stating that Green Card cover is provided. However, an actual Green Card is still a widely recognised document throughout Europe and is most likely to be recognised and understood should you have an accident. If you wish to have a physical Green Card, your insurance company should be able to send you one upon request. The Motor Insurers' Bureau (www.mib.org.uk) administers the Green Card system in the UK but does not provide Green Card insurance.

Police or ministry check points occur all over Europe and a vigilant motorist will notice that oncoming vehicles usually flash to indicate the presence of a speed trap or check point. Vehicles that are pulled over will be inspected and the officials will be looking for the essential items listed at the beginning of Chapter 4 as well as any vehicle defects. Ensure you are aware of all requirements before you tour; for example, in winter Germany requires all vehicles to be fitted with winter or all season tyres. Speed camera detectors or satellite navigators with speed camera locations are banned in several countries, such as France. The AA website provides details of vehicle requirements, drink drive limits, radar detector laws, seatbelt laws and fines at www.theaa.com/motoring_advice/overseas/index.html.

Signs may indicate speed cameras. Many countries prohibit the use of speed camera detection equipment and the speed camera function should be disabled on your satellite navigator.

Police issuing charges for vehicle or driving offences will normally collect fines on-the-spot.

The EU CAR Information Service (EUCARIS) enables vehicle and driving licence data to be exchanged within the EU. The level of data provided varies country to country but is increasing, see www.eucaris.net/participation for up-to-date information. In February 2015, Belgium, France, Germany, Italy, the Netherlands, and Switzerland were exchanging vehicle and owner data for the enforcement of traffic violations and unpaid tolls. Outstanding fines do not go away, so if you return to a country and are stopped by the police it is likely that unpaid fines and additional late payment penalties may be applied. EU countries may request through the courts the contact details of any offender who has fines over €70.

Vehicle Recovery

Broken-down motorhomes may not be able to be recovered by standard recovery trucks due to the motorhomes weight and the rear overhang. The overhang normally prevents towing on a hydraulic lift system, where the front wheels are lifted off the ground, as the rear of the motorhome could get damaged. Instead a vehicle designed for recovering commercial vehicles may have to be used. Rigid or rope towing systems may be suitable for a short distance as long as the towing vehicle is sufficiently large. Automatic vehicles cannot be towed unless the drive wheels are off the road. Some recovery companies will not recover vehicles they deem to be overweight. Whenever you contact your recovery company for assistance advise them of your vehicle's weight and dimensions.

Standard recovery trucks, like this one, may not be able to recover large motorhomes. Thankfully, campervans are no problem.

On Christmas day, whilst driving in Normandy, France, our brakes completely failed but we were able to stop safely. After phoning and making arrangements with our recovery company we were transported, along with the motorhome, to a garage and abandoned outside for the night. The next day the garage opened, inspected the brakes and ordered the parts. On the third day the €500 repairs were completed. The recovery company organised everything professionally and made sure that we were taken to a garage where someone spoke some English. We do feel that €500 was a lot for a replacement brake calliper and new rear brake shoes, but what choice did we have?

Breakdown recovery may be offered with motorhome insurance or it can be bought independently. Wherever you buy breakdown recovery, clearly state the dimensions and weight of your motorhome ensuring that they can and will recover it; you may wish to have this confirmed in writing. Confirm the territorial limits because some companies exclude some Green Card countries. Ensure you understand the level of UK and European breakdown assistance provided. Roadside assistance may not be available in Europe and the motorhome may be taken to the nearest garage regardless of the fault. Confirm how many continuous days Continental travel are covered. Some policies offer a trip total and annual total. The following chart provides a snapshot of some restrictions applied by recovery companies.

Organisation	Duration restrictions	Weight restrictions	Width restrictions	Length restrictions	Height restrictions	Territorial limitations
Caravan Club Mayday	None	None	None	None	None	UK
Caravan Club Red Pennant	None	3,850kg	2.3m – 7'6"	7.32m – 24'0"	3m – 9'10"	EU +
AA UK	None	3,500kg	2.3m – 7'6"	None	None	UK
AA Europe	350 days	3,500kg	2.3m – 7'6"	7m – 23'0"	3m – 9'10"	EU +
RAC UK	None	3,500kg	2.3m – 7'6"	5.5m – 18'0"	None	UK
RAC Europe	90 days	3,500kg	2.55m – 8'4"	7m – 23'0"	3m – 9'10"	EU +
Camping and Caravanning Club, Arrival (RAC)	90 days	None	None	None	None	EU +
Green Flag	90 days	3,500kg	2.55m – 8'4"	7m – 23'0"	3m – 9'10"	EU +

The Caravan Club's Red Pennant Overseas Motoring Cover can be adjusted to suit individual member requirements at a cost. They insure motorhomes up to 15 years old, www.caravanclub.co.uk, Tel: 01342 326944. The AA charges an older vehicle supplement for all vehicles over six years old, www.theaa.com, Tel: 0800 0852721. The RAC offers cover for vehicles up to 11 years old at the start of the journey, www.rac.co.uk, Tel: 0800 0156000. Green Flag cover vehicles less than 16 years old, www.greenflag.com, Tel: 0845 2462766.

Personal Health And Wellbeing

The European Health Insurance Card (EHIC) allows UK citizens to access medical care at state hospitals within the EEC. You may have to pay for treatment at reduced cost and then seek reimbursement in the UK. The EHIC replaces and invalidates all previous E111 forms. The EHIC can be applied for online at www.ehic.org.uk or a form can be acquired from the Post Office. The EHIC card is valid for five years and can be renewed up to six months before the expiry date.

The EHIC does not replace travel insurance because it will not cover the cost of returning you to the UK, mountain rescue, or any treatment carried out by private healthcare organisations. Personal medical insurance is not a legal requirement, but it is advisable to have when travelling, especially if you are not an EU citizen or if you intend to travel outside of the EU. Independent motorhomers should remember there is no tour rep or travel company support.

Ensure your personal insurance provides for:
- Flying you home if medically required.
- Flying out relatives if you are ill or imprisoned.
- Repatriating your body.
- Providing search and rescue.
- Providing adequate medical cover.
- Flying you home for a relative's funeral (although you are unlikely to be more than three days' drive from the UK).
- Providing cover for sports and activities, such as bicycling, walking, swimming, or travelling in someone else's car. Could you go horse riding, skiing, windsurfing, or canoeing? Dangerous sports are covered if required, but be aware of what is not covered.

Go Motorhoming and Campervanning

People with existing medical conditions can obtain insurance from All Clear to Travel, visit www.allcleartravel.co.uk, Tel: 0845 2505350. Saga covers pre-existing medical conditions and states no upper age limit, visit www.saga.co.uk, Tel: 0800 0158055. Free Spirit Travel Insurance provide travel insurance for people over 80 years old, visit www.freespirittravelinsurance.com, Tel: 0845 230 5000. www.travelhealth.co.uk details other insurers.

Many high street companies provide travel insurance, but we recommend you look at comprehensive travel insurance policies available to independent travellers. STA Travel provides travel insurance for people 65 or younger, www.statravel.co.uk, Tel: 0333 3210099. Endsleigh will insure people under 65 years old for 365 days' travel and 65-74 year olds for 183 days per year, visit www.endsleigh.co.uk, Tel: 0800 0283571. Saga offers travel insurance to people over 50 and has no upper age limit, visit www.saga.co.uk, Tel: 0800 0158055. Be aware that these policies may be voided if you return to the UK for more than 24 hours. So if you are planning to return, only book insurance to that point, it can always be extended if your plans change. Check the small print to see if your insurance is invalidated by any activities, such as consuming alcohol. Generally travel cover is not provided in any country designated as a 'war zone' or 'unsafe', so check the Foreign Office website regularly (www.gov.uk/fco) for details of countries that British citizens are advised not to travel to.

We recommend that you have vaccinations against infections spread via faecal matter. Cross-contamination can occur at combined toilet emptying and water collection points, both at campsites and Motorhome Stopovers. We have witnessed, all too often, the spout of a toilet cassette being placed over the fresh water tap during rinsing. The following diseases

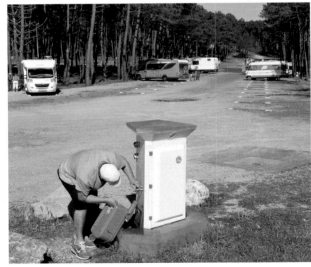

Two taps reduce the risk of cross-contamination.

Fill your fresh water tank from taps marked 'Drinking Water'.

can be spread via faecal matter and can be vaccinated against: Hepatitis A, Cholera, Polio, and you should confirm that your tetanus and diphtheria vaccinations are up-to-date. These injections are usually free on the NHS and some are simply boosters required every 10 years as part of the NHS vaccination programme if you were vaccinated as a child.

Other diseases found in Europe that you might consider vaccinating against include Rabies, spread by animal bites, and Tick Borne Encephalitis, spread by tick bites and unpasteurised milk. Some vaccinations require a course of injections over a month or more and may have to be specially ordered. Any vaccination not available on the NHS can be bought from your doctor or a travel clinic, such as MASTA, visit www.masta-travel-health.com.

Europe has resident mosquitoes and, although these are unlikely to carry malaria, before you depart seek medical advice based on the countries you intend to visit, www.gov.uk/fco. Mosquito bites can be itchy and uncomfortable and they often develop into aggravated penny-sized reactions. Pack insect repellent, after bite, and antihistamines in your medical kit. Scandinavia, especially Finland, appears to have the most ferocious mosquitoes, but more Brits are bitten in Spain. A mosquito head cover is worth buying if visiting northern Scandinavia in summer. Individual country information and vaccination advice can be found at www.fitfortravel.nhs.uk and www.travelhealth.co.uk. Travel with sufficient prescription and over-the-counter medicines for your trip. Carry your prescription to provide evidence to authorities if required. You may be

Australian mozzie warning.

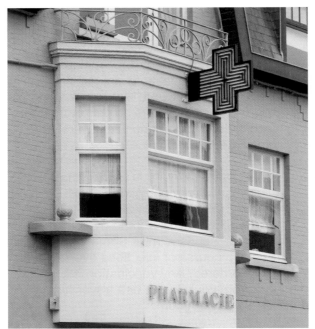
Pharmacies are usually indicated by an illuminated green cross.

able to buy drugs from pharmacies for self-medication if you know the active ingredient name. European pharmacists often sell what would be prescription medicines in the UK and will assist as much as language allows.

European pharmacies are clearly signed by a green cross or a blue Star of Life. Drugs are expensive in Germany and Italy and inexpensive in Greece, Spain, and Andorra. Medical advice is provided on www.nhs.uk. Campsite receptions and tourist information offices should provide contact details of local doctors. Explaining problems can be difficult so you may have to wait for an English-speaking doctor. People with pre-existing medical conditions may wish to identify this with jewellery displaying a Star of Life. UTAG produce USB drives designed to be worn around your neck or on your wrist, and a card version to carry in your wallet. The Star of Life symbol is clearly displayed and the USB drive can be loaded with your medical data and any other digital data, visit www.utagice.com for more details.

Finance, Budgeting And Keeping Costs Down

£250 is the minimum weekly budget required for two people actively touring with a motorhome. Restrained spending is required as this includes food, fuel, accommodation, repairs, tourism, literally everything except insurance. When touring Scandinavia, expect to spend £300 per week as the cost of living and unavoidable ferry crossings stretch the budget. To stay within these figures you will not be able to eat out often, go to every tourist site, or stay in campsites every night. If you stay on one campsite for an extended period you can expect to spend £150-£200 per week, around £750 per month. If your budget is tight, log your expenses daily in a cashbook; some people will find this interesting irrespective of budget. Working whilst travelling may be part of your plan, but it will take quite a lot of effort to find suitable work. Jobs generally fall into two categories: lifestyle jobs or short-term cash jobs. Neither is well paid, but lifestyle jobs allow the continuation of a lifestyle choice. Some campsite wardens work during the summer and tour the rest of the year or spend the winter in Spain. Campsite wardens work when everyone else is on holiday; they clean toilets, mow grass, do office work, and need good customer service skills. Detailed information about becoming a warden for The Caravan Club is available at www.caravanclub.co.uk. The Camping and Caravanning Club also has warden positions, www.campingandcaravanningclub.co.uk/aboutus/work-with-us/jobs, whilst privately owned campsites advertise jobs on www.ukcampsite.co.uk/jobs and www.caravan-jobfinder.co.uk.

House sitting may provide you with some income. HG Security employs motorhome owners to guard empty property. Training and certification is required for this job, visit www.hgsecurity.co.uk. Another website, www.mindmyhouse.com, matches house sitters with house owners. Most sitters offer their services for free and house owners are expected to cover reasonable utility costs. Jobs in the travel industry are generally very competitive and you will have to work very hard to become a paid writer in magazines. There are limited opportunities for guidebook inspectors and tour leaders for motorhome holidays, and it is advisable to contact the company you wish to work for directly to register your interest and availability.

People who like to be outside and do not mind hard work may consider fruit picking. Many farms in the UK need fruit pickers from June to October. Pickers are required in France to harvest grapes in the autumn and payment is around €50 per day including board and lodging, information can be found at www.pickingjobs.com. Organic farms worldwide take on voluntary workers in exchange for board and lodging, visit www.wwoof.net. www.seasonworkers.com advertises seasonal jobs such as ski instructor, chalet maid, or campsite cleaner. Entrepreneurial campers have run small businesses from their motorhomes, for example hairdressing, soft toy making, retailing electrical goods, and artists who paint scenes on motorhomes. Check with reception before you start working from your pitch. EU citizens can work freely in the EU, but visitors from outside the EU should check their visas.

Euros are the principal currency in Europe, even outside the euro zone, having replaced American dollars. If you intend to take travellers' cheques, ensure they are in euros to prevent double transactions. It is advisable to take a small amount of euros in cash when you depart the UK and keep a small amount of sterling for your return. Visa and MasterCard credit and debit cards are

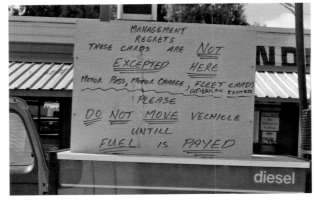

Visa and MasterCard are usually accepted, but American Express is rarely accepted in Europe. Who knows if this Road House in Western Australia accepts the cards that 'are NOT EXCEPTED'.

widely accepted in most countries, except the Netherlands and Germany. American Express is rarely accepted. There is no need to obtain large amounts of euros before you travel as ATMs, commonly known as cash machines, are widely available across Europe at service stations, banks and supermarkets. Most towns should have at least one ATM, but they are rare in villages or rural communities. Most ATMs offer a choice of languages, so the transaction can take place in English. Bank ATMs rarely charge for transactions, however those found in shops and fuel stations often do. A message is normally displayed detailing charges, so it's your choice. Withdrawing cash on your credit card will incur charges. Check that your bank cards will remain valid for the duration of your trip. Do not forget to pay your credit card's monthly bill by direct debit, or pay a lump sum into your credit card account before departure.

Spend a few hours checking the foreign currency bank charges and exchange rates offered by the high street banks. Frequent or long-term travellers could save considerable amounts of money by opening and using a favourable account, see www.metrobankonline.co.uk. Check for the following charges:

- Withdrawing money from a Continental ATM machine, ideally this should be free.
- Making a purchase using your debit/credit card, ideally this should be free.
- The exchange rate offered by the card. This will be a figure that changes

daily (sometimes hourly), ideally you want a rate better than the tourist rate. To check the figure offered by the bank you will need to check that figure against other currency providers, such as the Post Office or a travel agent on the same day.

- Ask if there are any additional charges, such as a commission charge for changing the money from sterling (£) to euros.

Pre-paid euro debit cards operate on a pay-as-you-go basis. When you top up, sterling is converted to euros and is spent using the debit card when abroad. This means that you can top up when exchange rates are favourable or use it as a saving method to help pay for your trip. This type of card may offer better exchange rates and charges than your current debit/credit card. Check if the pre-loaded card has an application fee or a top-up fee. Several companies offer pre-paid euro cards including www.caxtonfxcard.com, Tel: 0845 222 2639, and www.travelex.co.uk, Tel: 0845 8727627.

When entering non-euro currency countries, cash can usually be withdrawn from an ATM at the first town or fuel station. Do not panic as euros are often accepted near borders, although not necessarily at a good exchange rate. Careful cash withdrawal management will avoid the use of bureau de change and double transactions, for example changing sterling into euros into lev. Placing sole responsibility of money outside the euro zone to one person should avoid departing the country with money left over.

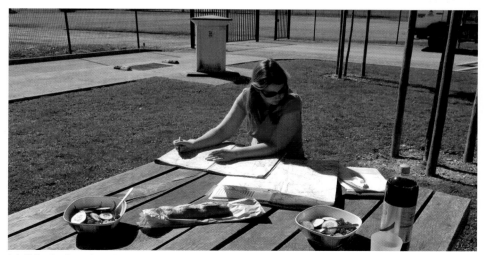

Meli finds time for trip planning during lunch.

Go Motorhoming and Campervanning

Supermarkets usually have the cheapest fuel.

Well-known tourist sites are often expensive and lesser-known sites are often free. Repeated occupations, strategic marriages, and millennia of cross-border trade have enabled copycat architecture across Europe. The Greek temples in Sicily rival those found in Greece, and there appears to be an 'English Garden' in every European country. Most people decide upon their destination first, but we believe that you should focus on what you are going to see and do day-to-day and let that guide you. Buy your tourist information guidebooks and do your research in advance. Choose the sites you wish to visit, and then plan your route to prevent unnecessary miles criss-crossing a country or continent. Free sites are detailed in country and, to a greater extent, regional guidebooks, whereas Europe-wide guidebooks will focus on the major tourist-trap attractions.

Generally, fuel is most expensive on the motorways and cheapest at supermarket fuel stations, with a difference of 10-15 cents. Access into supermarket fuel stations is often restricted due to height barriers, low canopies, or limited space, so proceed with caution. When approaching borders look at the number plates of cars in the fuel stations and supermarkets, this indicates which country has cheaper fuel or food. In southern Italy you have to be particularly vigilant as often the price advertised is only for the pump marked *Fia Dante*, the others can be up to 10 cents per litre more. Fuel also tends to be cheaper in principalities, such as Andorra and the Grand Duchy of Luxembourg. Diesel is predominantly cheaper than petrol in Europe. The Drive Alive website details current fuel prices across Europe, www.drive-alive.co.uk/fuel_prices_europe.html, and www.prix-carburants.gouv.fr shows fuel prices including LPG across France.

Unfortunately, the size of your motorhome will affect your budget. Motorhomes over 6m long or over 3,500kg can be considered large and heavy and additional charges often apply for pitches, tolls and ferries. Motorhomes with twin axles and or trailers also attract additional charges. In several European countries motorhomes over 3,500kg pay higher tolls,

Austria being a prime example, and failing to pay the correct fee can result in a large fine. To keep travel costs down, avoid toll roads and use the local roads instead. When money is tight, you can forget going to Norway because there is often no option but to pay tolls and catch ferries.

Large campsites normally have onsite shops, where, as you might expect, you pay for convenience. Some small campsites may sell only local wine or fresh bread, which you may have to order the night before. When you are staying at Motorhome Stopovers you should shop locally as much as possible, but when you are paying to stop at campsites this moral obligation is negated. Hypermarkets without height restricted parking are found Europe-wide so it is possible to stock up before going to campsites. Continental signing laws allow hypermarkets to provide directional signs from great distances, so they are easy to find. As in the UK, supermarket prices vary and some offer discounts on fuel when you shop in store. Buying long-life products, such as UHT milk, reduces the need to shop regularly. Make the most of your fridge by removing bulky packaging. Prevent messy spills by keeping items in the fridge in sealed containers; plastic take away containers are ideal. Ensure that milk containers, etc, have pop down or screw tops rather than a tear off opening, although a peg can be used to seal the opening. In many Continental supermarkets, especially Scandinavia, they either charge for or do not have carrier bags. Fold up cloth bags are stronger than carrier bags and more practical when walking or cycling with shopping.

Communication

English and German are the two main tourist languages spoken across Europe. Most campsite receptions and tourist offices will have an English speaker. The Dutch and the Swiss are very useful for translation as they generally speak both English and German. The Italians will speak to you whether or not they speak English or you speak Italian. Out of respect, you should learn how to say hello in the country's language, then ask if anyone speaks English. You may also wish to learn how to say that you have not learnt any more of their language. Start a conversation this way, no matter how bad your pronunciation or limited your vocabulary, and people respond well, especially if they are hesitant to speak English. If you intend to travel predominantly in one country, then learning that language would be useful. If you cannot attend a language course, then language CDs will give you basic knowledge and provide entertainment whilst driving. In any country it is worth learning the basics of 'hello', 'goodbye', 'please', 'thank you', and 'I would like'. Many guidebooks provide these basic words, nevertheless buying a language dictionary is money well spent.

The most reliable way to receive post whilst abroad is to have it sent to a campsite or domestic address. Vicarious-Shop.com sends books by airmail all over Europe and the success rate is better than 99 per cent. The unreliable element is the delivery time as some books are received within two days and some take one month. There is no pattern to the delivery times so make sure you plan for delays. Spain has the most unreliable post and often 'returns to sender' any mail with an incorrect address or postcode. Post can be sent *'Poste Restante'* to a post office of your choice, but Vicarious-Shop.com has found this less reliable. Poste Restante letters need to be addressed to Poste Restante first, then your surname, followed by your Christian name, and finally the address of your chosen post office. Poste Restante needs to be substituted with *Postlagernd* in Germany and Austria, *Fermo Posta* in Italy and *Lista de Correos* in Spain. Letters and parcels are filed at the receiving post office under the first letter of the first word, which may be your surname, first name, title or any other possibility, making them difficult to track down. A passport is required for identification and some post offices may charge upon collection. Items will only be held for one month.

Mobile phones and internet connection have merged into one fast moving subject. We are grateful that Adam from www.motorhomewifi.com was willing to give up his time to help us update this section.

There are three ways to obtain an internet connection from your motorhome: mobile (3/4G) cellular networks, WiFi and satellite internet.

Laptop and dongle.

Connecting to mobile (3/4G) cellular networks requires a enabled SIM card and a device such as a smart phone or tablet with a SIM card slot. Smart phones often have the ability to broadcast a portable WiFi signal. Pocket-sized mobile WiFi devices (brand name MiFi) work in a similar way and also broadcast a secure WiFi connection that multiple devices can use simultaneously, even whilst driving as long as 3/4G is available. Some devices can be connected to external window or roof mounted 3/4G antennas for improved signal in poor coverage areas.

Ensure that you buy unlocked phones or mobile WiFi devices that

Free internet access is available from McDonald's in the UK, France and Spain.

are roaming enabled so that you can use them in any country and use SIM cards from any network provider or country. Calls, text, and data roaming charges vary between network operators, especially outside of EU and EEA countries. In 2014 the European Parliament passed a bill that should end all roaming charges commencing 15th December 2015. However the European Council failed to pass the bill into law. At the time of publishing, roaming charges remain until the 2018 review. Currently European roaming charges are capped at: 18p per minute for an EU-EU call, 4p per minute for any incoming call, 5p per text message sent, and 19p per MB of data used. In addition, users must be alerted if they reach £48 worth of use within a 30-day billing cycle and must opt in to continue. There are many roaming packages available, but most have exclusions that prohibit long-term roaming use. Almost without exception, purchasing a 'roaming package' removes the expenditure cap protection, thus care is needed. Check to see

if your device allows you to monitor data use. Data monitoring apps are available. You are advised to turn 'data' off when it is not required.

UK operator Three offers 'feel at home' packages that allow you to use a set amount of your minutes, texts and data at the same rates as the UK when roaming in Austria, Denmark, Finland, France, Italy, Ireland, Norway, Spain (from 1st April 2015), Sweden

Internet booster antennas can increase WiFi connection range.

and Switzerland. In addition Pay-As-You-Go (PAYG) mobile broadband SIMs are available offering 1GB of data in 30 days for £10.49, 3GB in 3 months for £20.49 and 12GB in 12 months for £70.49. Motorhome WiFi keeps an up-to-date list of all providers and their roaming charges on its homepage, www.motorhomewifi.com.

There are network providers that specialise in roaming. Toggle Mobile offers free incoming calls in specified countries and outgoing calls start at 3p per minute. At the time of publishing, roaming data was 15p per MB. Visit www.togglemobile.co.uk for the latest rates. Europe-wide data only packages are available from www.globalgig.com.

You can buy local SIM cards whilst abroad but it is essential that your hardware is 'unlocked'. Some countries require you to be a resident or at least give a local address. Try to find a retailer that can explain the tariff options and provide you with the correct APN settings. If possible, get them to help you during SIM registration.

Connecting to WiFi can be free at bars, restaurants, and fast food chains, such as McDonald's. Campsites increasingly offer WiFi hotspots and unsecured networks are often accessible, but the strength of signal may be inadequate when you are using a device inside your motorhome. A WiFi booster can greatly improve the strength of the signal. Plug and play booster antennas are available from www.motorhomewifi.com.

Directional panel antenna for WiFi connection. Photo: www.motorhomewifi.com.

You have the choice of omni-directional antennas or line-of-sight directional panels. Omni antennas pick up signals from all directions thus are the easiest to use. Suction cup mountings enable you to temporarily stick the booster to the side of your motorhome. Brackets for permanent installation are available. Caution should be used when connecting to unsecured signals since you may not be able to identify the source or the legality of using someone else's connection. Becoming part of a WiFi community will further increase your likelihood of finding a connection. FON (www.fon.com) is the largest of such and BT Broadband subscribers

(5 million) as well as SFR in France (4 million) are opted in by default. Adam is frequently asked if it is possible to improve WiFi connections to allow streaming of UK TV channels whilst in Spain. Doing so requires a large amount of data, as much as 500MB per hour, thus is cost prohibitive on cellular networks. Very few campsites will have WiFi networks that can meet customer demand, so streaming should be considered a bonus and not an expectation.

Internet connection via satellites is possible and works in much the same as satellite TV, and one dish can be used to do both jobs. The main advantage of internet via satellite is that it offers the most effective and reliable service throughout Europe because it is not reliant on WiFi or 3/4G signals. Receiving systems start at £3,300 plus fitting.

Various data packages are available. Consider frequency of use, connection charges and fair use caps that may stop you streaming endless TV. The satellite footprint covers most of Europe, but does not cover Eastern Europe and most of Scandinavia, although it does cover Denmark, Iceland, and Scotland. Contact Motorhome WiFi, RoadPro or Conrad Anderson for further information and current prices.

Once connected to the internet you can communicate by email, via social media or by updating a blog, all of which are free to use. Internet video calls are also free through VoIP (Voice over Internet Protocol) an internet-based telephone service. There may be small annual subscription charges for membership and voicemail. In addition you can buy subscriptions that allow you to call landlines around the world for free. If you choose to subscribe to a telephone number, anyone can call you at standard rate. Calls to landlines and mobile phones are from 1.2-15p per minute. We use a VoIP service through Skype, www.skype.com, and have successfully used it abroad when we have accessed the internet through our laptop. Several other companies including BT, www.BT.com, also offer VoIP.

If Things Go Wrong

Before you travel visit the Foreign and Commonwealth Office website (www.gov.uk/fco, Tel: 0845 8502829) to check their advice about the countries you intend to visit. Travelling to countries identified as not recommended should be avoided. People touring should aim to view this website regularly to ensure they do not end up driving into an unexpected local situation.

112 is an EU-wide phone number that connects you to the police, ambulance or fire brigade; multilingual operators are often employed. The 112 number is free of charge and no roaming charges apply. If you need assistance abroad, you should contact your nearest embassy. A list of British embassies can be found at www.gov.uk/government/world/organisations, or by calling the Consular Assistance team in London (Tel: 0044 (0)20 70081500 available 24/7). The embassy can: issue replacement passports, provide assistance if you are a victim of crime or you are hospitalised, provide details of lawyers, doctors, interpreters and funeral directors, contact your friends and family and help by liaising with your medical insurance company. The embassy will not: pay for or provide medical treatment, interfere with criminal or civil court proceedings, get you out of prison, investigate crimes, search for missing people, or interfere in another country's immigration policy if you do not have a visa or your passport is invalid.

Your embassy, or other authorities, may require documentation from you that may no longer be accessible to you. We strongly recommend that you ask someone that you trust to become your HQ (headquarters) to manage your affairs, receive your mail and be on the end of the phone if you need anything. Provide them with electronic copies and colour photocopies of all your important documents, which should be kept flat in a folder in case they need to be faxed. Insurance companies should be given the name of the person who you wish to act on your behalf. We also recommend that you take copies with you or store them securely online. Copies of the documents listed below are to be kept by HQ and the originals in the motorhome safe:

- A colour photocopy of passports and the original birth certificate of each passenger to be left with HQ. In the event of passports being lost, these documents are required by the British Consulate.
- Copies of your European Health Insurance Card and medical insurance. Details of your blood group, vaccinations, any medical conditions and copies of any prescriptions.
- Copies of all documentation regarding the ownership of your vehicle, MOTs, breakdown recovery and insurance. Include copies of relevant driving licences.
- Banking details so that money can be transferred to you if necessary. Ideally leave some money with HQ to cover any expenses and some for contingencies.
- Leave a copy of next of kin details and phone numbers of anyone you

may need to contact while you are away, for instance your alarm fitters, warranties, motorhome dealer, etc.
- Consider leaving copies, or locations, of wills and power of attorney documents.
- Your planned route and the countries you intend to visit.

Boaters will be familiar with the concept of a grab bag. These contain equipment needed when abandoning ship. The motorhomer's grab bag should have a photocopy of all vital documents: passports, health and vehicle documents with emergency phone numbers, a small amount of cash, and a few days worth of any medication you may need. Store important phone numbers in your mobile phone such as emergency medical helpline, travel insurance, and vehicle recovery and insurance companies. Putting a paper copy of these numbers in your purse or wallet is also advisable. When engaging in sport, such as walking, cycling, or skiing, carry your EHIC cards and a copy of your travel insurance.

Both personal GPS tracking devices and mobile phones can relay your position to selected people or organisations, like the emergency services, or to social media platforms like Facebook or Twitter. The Spot Satellite Messenger is a personal GPS tracking device that can send the GPS coordinates of your location to as many as 10 contacts. For fun you could set it to pinpoint your locations on Google maps so friends can log in and view your journey. It also has a help request button, which sends a message to a designated mobile phone number, and an SOS button to relay your location to the emergency services. Visit www.findmespot.eu/en.

Jean Sear and her husband were involved in a road accident when he fainted at the wheel of their 21' Elddis Voyager on the A9 in France. The motorhome drifted into a concrete bollard at 50mph. Both Jean and her husband survived the crash, but their insurance company declared their motorhome a write-off. Jean offers the following advice:

- Swap details with other people involved in the accident, and take many photos and video of the scene and people around you.
- Contact your insurers as soon as possible and get a reference number and a free-phone number in case you need to phone again.
- There is a time limit for the submission of a claim, ask what this is and stick to it.
- Check the amount your insurers will pay for B&B. You may choose to spend more.

- Keep in phone contact with your insurer throughout.
- You will need your EHIC and travel insurance documents if taken to hospital.
- If the hospital gives you verbal advice about what not to do as a result of your injuries (i.e. driving), get it in writing so that you can use it as evidence when you make a claim.
- If medical staff have advised you not to drive, inform the insurance company to organise the repatriation of your motorhome.
- Keep track of your motorhome's location. At some point you will need to visit it to obtain documentation and belongings.
- Record in a notebook the name of everyone you speak to, as well as the date and time of the conversation. Verbal agreements must be confirmed in writing. Keep every original receipt, regardless of whether the item is 'excluded' from the insurance policy.
- Defensive driving should be practised at all times. Knowing the local road rules as well as observing road signs will prevent you making driving errors.

Modern motorhomes are capable of being driven at normal road speeds. Despite this, most motorhomers drive their motorhomes slower than the rest of the traffic. In theory this appears safer, but in practice impatient motorists take unnecessary risks trying to overtake slow vehicles. If you wish to drive slower than the normal road speed, consider choosing quieter minor roads. Remember to pull over frequently to let vehicles behind get on their way. Driving with dipped headlights during daytime makes the vehicle more visible and has had a significant impact in reducing accidents in countries where it is compulsory. Although the Highway Code describes flashing fellow motorists as a warning, being flashed in the UK usually means a motorist is giving way or letting you out at a junction; on the Continent flashing is definitely intended as a warning. Never pull out in front of a vehicle that flashes you as it is probably travelling at great speed and is not going to give way under any circumstances.

Try to avoid driving in the dark on unfamiliar roads. A-Class motorhomes offer excellent daytime visibility, but at night reflections on the glass can be quite hard to see through and this is compounded the further you are away from the windscreen. Add rain, condensation or mist and you will have to concentrate very hard to see the road. Pedestrians may use the hard shoulder as a footpath; this is especially common in eastern Europe and Morocco. On unlit roads, it appears obligatory for pedestrians to wear black. Scooters, farm, and horse-drawn vehicles may be travelling against

Snow ploughs keep main routes open. Photo: Andy Glasgow.

the traffic flow. Not all countries have effective road drainage and rain leads to flash flooding and minor landslips. Driving through deep puddles is stressful and, in most cases, avoidable if you wait for the rain to pass. All countries endeavour to keep the main routes open during winter with grit and snow ploughs, although snow chains may still be required. Minor roads may not have snow cleared at all. Ensure you are prepared for every eventuality if you deviate off the main routes or there is any possibility of a navigation error. Avoid driving into large cities where possible, as they can be busy, confusing and stressful experiences. Is it really worth the double parking of Rome and the chaos of Athens when you can park outside the town and use public transport to get in?

Some unscrupulous people see foreigners and foreign vehicles as an opportunity to make a quick buck. Criminals normally use distraction techniques to gain entry into your motorhome or relieve you of your wallet, handbag, or cash. We strongly recommend that you watch as many programs of the BBC's 'The Real Hustle' as you can because the scams always use similar techniques, and once you learn to recognise them you stop being a vulnerable 'mark'. We have previously written that motorway service and rest areas in southern France and Spain are the most likely place to be broken into. The same area, especially the main coast route, is the most common place for the following distraction scams to take place. One scam has smartly dressed people in a reasonable car frantically waving and pointing at the rear of the motorhome. Having encouraged the driver to stop they pull in behind and get out to identify the fault. A lit oily rag is thrown under the motorhome, the smoke and commotion is intended to get the occupants out of the motorhome, so a companion can rob valuables or steal the motorhome. The only advice that can be given is if you think it's a trick, it probably is; so making it obvious that you're not an easy target is your best defence. You should always travel with all doors and windows locked. The smell of hot brakes or burning rubber is very obvious; check mirrors, look out of the windows, see if other motorists are looking at you strangely, and switch on your rear view camera if fitted. Then give the suspects the international OK sign and beckon them to go on their way. Filming or photographing them, and making it obvious that you are

Go Motorhoming and Campervanning

doing so, will probably encourage them on their way. Remember, most mobiles now have cameras so any small object will look convincing. If you do decide you need to stop, pull into a service station and stop outside the shop or restaurant or in view of a CCTV camera. Try not to pull over until they, and any other suspect cars, are well away. Exit the vehicle calmly and lock doors before proceeding to investigate the problem.

At tourist sites, you may be asked to pay security/parking by an unsavoury character or child. This is normal in Morocco, but is likely to be a scam in the rest of Europe. Presumably you are paying them not to damage your vehicle. It is up to you whether you pay or take the risk. Just try not to let it ruin your visit, and report it if possible. This has only happened to us in Sicily at the Valley of the Temples. Should you ever be asked by official-looking people to have your money checked, 'as there has been a spate of forgeries', don't fall for it. Simply say you will call in at the police station.

Before picking up a hitchhiker, consider the dangers associated with inviting a stranger into your motorhome. Will they harm you? Damage any property? Invite themselves for lunch? Or decide that they like travelling by motorhome and do not want to leave, especially if you have a spare bed. You may end up transporting illegal immigrants, especially if you intend to cross a border.

> *Handbags are like gift wrapped presents to thieves and handbag theft is the most common crime reported to Vicarious Media. Just in case this needs spelling out: Do not take a handbag with you.*

Personal security is very important when you are out and about. Always present yourself as an unsuitable victim. Handbags are like gift wrapped presents to thieves and handbag theft is the most common crime reported to Vicarious Media. Just in case this needs spelling out: Do not take a handbag with you. Although only a very small percentage of our customers are involved in this type of crime, we advise that you keep all valuables and documentation locked in a safe within the motorhome or, when passports are required as ID, in a money pouch under clothing. If you cannot live without your handbag, ensure it can be securely closed and place the strap over your head and across your body so that you can keep the bag in front of you. Do not take or wear expensive jewellery unless you are prepared to lose it. If handbags are Christmas presents for criminals, then rucksacks and bum-bags are birthday presents. If you must take one, avoid carrying valuables in them.

A money belt is the only way to keep cash and cards safe when in crowded places, as long as you keep it under clothing. Usually money belts are flesh-coloured lightweight cloth belts with a zipped pocket. They are very discreet when worn around the waist and we recommend that you put it down the front of your trousers under your belt. When out and about keep most of your cash along with passports, and cards in the money belt and use a mugger's wallet for every day purchases. A mugger's wallet is a sacrificial wallet or purse that you keep in a zipped pocket. Make it look as real as possible by putting in some expired or cancelled cards, a photo, some receipts, business cards, and enough cash to get you through the day. Always use this wallet, otherwise it will not be convincing, but especially at vulnerable places such as public transport or tourist attraction kiosks. If someone attempts to mug or pickpocket you, they have something to steal that you are prepared to lose. Hopefully it will be over quickly and no harm done.

Capital cities, large towns, and busy tourist sites are the most likely places to be followed then mugged or pickpocketed. Always be aware of your situation, especially people brushing up against you or engaging you in conversation, for example asking directions, for change, or for a light. If you feel someone is in your personal space, step away and don't feel embarrassed about offending them. If you think you are being followed, stick to populated areas, vary your walking pace, and stop to look in shop windows. Try to deter your follower, get them in front of you, and if necessary go into a café or get into a taxi. A useful trick if you lose each other or you are alerting your partner to a concern you may have is to decide on a code whistle or song, which is used only for these occasions. This can be a little embarrassing at first; we always use it in the supermarket, not because we feel we are going to be robbed, but somebody always wanders off. Carrying pepper spray or a baton can be tempting, but the problem with weapons is they could be used against you and there are legal implications. All types of travel incur some risk. Remember, motorhome-related crime is rare and pickpocketing and handbag snatching are avoidable.

Window covers may be taking security too seriously.

Vicarious Shop

CHAPTER 6 – Where To Stay

Motorhomers travelling in Europe have hundreds of thousands of places to stop overnight, from roadside lay-bys, to motorhome-only parking areas, to all-singing, all-dancing campsites. Only motorhomers have this freedom and freedom is the essence of motorhoming.

Campsites

Campsites may also be called caravan sites, campgrounds, touring parks, or campings. Despite the confusion of names, most sites will accommodate tents, caravans, and motorhomes. There are over 30,000 campsites across Europe, enough to stay at a different one every night for the next 82 years. One third, 10,500, of all European campsites are located in France. Campsites range from huge five-star holiday complexes to tiny campsites offering basic, affordable camping.

Small campsites, often referred to as 'Mini Camping', range from gardens or farms to municipally-provided camping areas. Most have the bare necessities of water collection and disposal, and are similar to Certified

The directions said: just follow the camping signs.

Sites/Locations administered by the clubs in the UK. Pitch fees range from €5-€10 per night. Farm camping is popular in France and has a supporting scheme called 'Bienvenue à la Ferme', www.bienvenue-a-la-ferme.com. French *Aire Naturelle* campsites are similar to UK Certified Locations/Sites, but are open only for the summer. Netherlands, Denmark and Germany have plenty of small, rural campsites often connected to farms or restaurants.

Trees create shade, but low branches can impede large motorhomes. Lech Camping, Bavaria, Germany.

Large, privately-run campsites are common in Europe, and these have similar facilities to the large commercial campsites found in the UK. They are likely to have: swimming pools, bars, restaurants, onsite activities, laundries, and multiple toilet blocks. British caravanners that have become accustomed to The Caravan Club's wardenised, manicured campsites will be disappointed when they go abroad. Pitches in southern Europe are devoid of grass and are normally surfaced with fine gravel or sand. The reasonable fire gap maintained between units on UK campsites is not a standard in Europe and no space is wasted. Trees normally delimit the pitches and they provide useful shade in August, conversely they make pitches dark, cold, and undesirable during winter. Trees and sunshades also create vehicle navigation obstacles and tight turns, which may be a problem if you have a large or tall motorhome. Pitch allocation can become a chaotic situation out of peak season if the campsite becomes self-regulated by the campers.

The majority of European campsites cater for caravans pitched for the season, often at the expense of touring pitches. Construction starts in March when season pitch users heave huge twin-axle caravans onto pitches, except in Italy where small, ancient caravans are pitched. Then the awning is erected and possibly a gazebo and a tarp to fill in the gaps. This tented space is carpeted or decked and a removal van load of stuff is

Home from home.

squeezed in. It really does include the kitchen sink, fridge freezer, kettle, oven, TV, and lounge furniture. Any remaining outside space is claimed and maintained by a white picket fence. Then a second removal van load of garden equipment is delivered including decking, rolls of turf, streetlights, BBQ, and all sorts of unnecessary stuff. These pitches are disassembled in September and October in some campsites, whilst others stay up for years making sections of the campsite resemble shantytowns.

Summer-only campsites normally open at Easter and close at the end of September. French campsites may not open until May and close the second week of September. Booking pitches in advance is not necessary for most European campsites except in high season, which includes bank/school holidays, and the last week in July until the third week in August. Even then, some campsites retain touring pitches or squeeze you in somewhere. July is high season in Scandinavia and popular winter campsites in Spain and Portugal have a second high season from December to February. Ski resorts across Europe have campsites that are open throughout the ski season.

Long-stay pitches can really add to the ambiance.

Go Motorhoming and Campervanning

Campsite pitch fees vary depending on the season, location and facilities, but expect to pay €20-€30 per night. There is no guarantee that expensive campsites are better than the cheap ones, or that higher star ratings relate to a better environment. Many campsites itemise their bills, for example: motorhome (small, medium, and large),

Ski resorts often have campsites that stay open all year. Camping Punt Muragi, Swizterland. Photo: Andy Glasgow.

awning, car, trailer, moped, person, children, pets, electricity (priced in a 3A, 6A and 16A scale), and supplements per person for environment and tourist tax. You may also have to pay extra to use the swimming pool, tennis courts, showers, hot water and have to supply your own toilet paper! These costs can add up and can make what appears to be a cheap campsite expensive. Normally pitches have to be vacated between 10am-midday and booking in starts from 2pm, departing late or arriving early can incur additional fees.

Campsites may offer a discount for long stays and campsite chains may offer loyalty schemes. Three companies offer Europe-wide low season discount camping schemes that generally exclude the last two weeks of July and the first three weeks of August. All three schemes offer fixed-price camping based on two people per night, including their camping unit, electricity, and a pet. Additional charges for local taxes such as tourist or environmental may apply. No booking is necessary, but if you wish to book in advance and want to use a discount scheme, you must make this clear at the time of booking.

27 EMPLACEMENTS	
Tarifs	
Adultes	2,95€
Enfants	2,00€
Emplacement	3,30€
Véhicules	2,20€
Electricité	3,25€
Garage mort	4,30€
Camping-car	
Emplacement électrique	12,50€
Emplacement + 2 adultes	10,50€
Borne de service	2,00€

Campsite fees may be itemised.

Touring Cheque and Camping Cheque sell pre-paid, time bound vouchers that can be redeemed at participating campsites. These cheques are ideal if you know exactly which participating campsite you are going to and for how long. In 2015, Touring Cheque had 114 participating campsites and Camping Cheques had 661 spread thinly all over Europe. This represents a problem for people on tour unless you are prepared to drive a long way to a participating campsite. Touring Cheques, www.touringcheque.co.uk, Tel: 08448 444111, cost £13.50 and Camping Cheques, www.campingcheque.co.uk, Tel: 01580 214002, cost €14.95 each (per night). Cheques are in either paper form or electronic format stored on a Silver or Gold Camping Cheque card. Some campsites offer additional discounts including seven nights for six cheques, three weeks for 14 cheques or 60 nights for 30 cheques. Camping Cheques are accepted at a few campsites during July and August. Check the small print in the back of the Camping Cheque sites guide as it may be possible to return cheques for replacement immediately after they expire.

We purchased 30 Camping Cheques in 2003, planning to use them on our year-long tour of Europe. When we returned in 2004, we still had 10 cheques left despite going out of our way to use them. We found the campsites were in the wrong locations for us, or when we turned up found that it was cheaper to pay cash, or we stayed on campsites that offered four nights for three cheques. Over the next six years we managed to use a few, and sent expired cheques back to Camping Cheque for replacement. Each time we sent the cheques back one was taken for administration. This continued until February 2010 when, despite returning the expired cheques to Camping Cheque, they failed to return any cheques to us. We were not bothered by this because we had learnt that we are never in the right place at the right time to use them.

The ACSI CampingCard is the largest Europe-wide discount camping scheme. In 2015 there were 2,940 participating campsites and each year hundreds more are added. The CampingCard is valid for one calendar year and is published annually in mid December. To obtain the card you must purchase the ACSI CampingCard guidebooks listing the campsites. The card presses out of the cover of Part 2. A mini atlas showing the site locations is found in the back of Part 1. There is no membership, upfront fees or further administration apart from writing your name and address on the back of the card. If you do not use the scheme, it has only cost you the price of a guidebook.

Users present the card at reception of the participating campsites and pay the receptionists either €12, €14, €16 or €18 per night, as identified in the guidebook. Some campsites offer free nights, for example stay seven and pay for six. The ACSI CampingCard is available from the Vicarious Shop, www.Vicarious-Shop.com, Tel: 0131 208 3333.

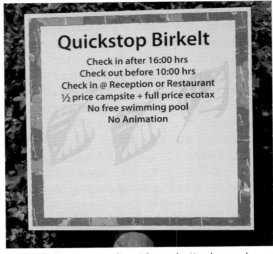

Quickstop Birkelt

Check in after 16:00 hrs
Check out before 10:00 hrs
Check in @ Reception or Restaurant
½ price campsite + full price ecotax
No free swimming pool
No Animation

A Quick Stop campsite at Larochette, Luxembourg.

Quick Stop camping is offered at selected campsites in some countries, particularly Denmark, Italy and Luxembourg. Motorhomers who arrive after 4pm and leave before 10am pay a reduced fee. The tourist office usually has details of Quick Stop campsites. There is a similar scheme operating in Spain called Formula Camper Andalucia, www.formulacamperandalucia.com. Use of the facilities is often restricted to the bare necessities. When booking in ensure that the receptionist has written down that you are paying the 'Quick Stop' price, except in Italy where it is called 'Camper Stop'.

Choosing a campsite remotely can be a difficult task. Where possible, use guidebooks from publishers that send inspectors to the campsites. Some websites allow customer comment, although you will have to learn how to interpret the comments. We have already explained that freedom is the essence of motorhoming, so instead of choosing a campsite and then fitting a holiday around it, why not decide what you want to do and then find campsites near to or suitable for the activity? Avoid advanced booking except in high season or possibly for your first night away to give you reassurance. Obtain country-specific guidebooks when you intend to travel in just one or two countries, also see the country guides on www.go-motorhoming.co.uk. When you are touring the whole of Europe the ACSI DVD is priceless, as long as you have a computer to run it on. The ACSI DVD is a searchable database of nearly 9,000 campsites that you load onto your computer, thus no internet connection is needed to search the database. Every campsite is inspected every year so the information is reliable. The Caravan Club Touring guides are popular paperback books.

that cover the whole of Europe. The information is customer submitted and can be up to six years old. Vicarious Shop stocks the guides mentioned above and numerous campsite guides for countries across Europe. For a complete product list visit www.Vicarious-Shop.com, Tel: 0131 2083333. Despite careful planning, you may arrive at your intended campsite only to find that you do not like it. Do not stay for the sake of it; there are plenty of other places to stay, so just move on.

Looking around a campsite before booking in is common practice in Europe and no one will be offended if you choose not to stay. Park near the entrance without obstructing it, enquire about price, and let reception know that you want to walk, or if it is big, drive around the site. Once you get used to being your own campsite inspector you quickly notice the important things. Out of season many of the facilities will be shut. It is not uncommon for the restaurant to be closed, the swimming pool to be drained in early September regardless of the weather, and the facilities may not be clean. A dirty campsite with limited facilities can feel very expensive. The chances are you will be allowed to select your own pitch and this can be more difficult than it appears when you consider satellite reception, hours of sunlight, noise, pitch gradient, and distance to facilities including water point and electric hook-up. Once you have chosen your pitch, return

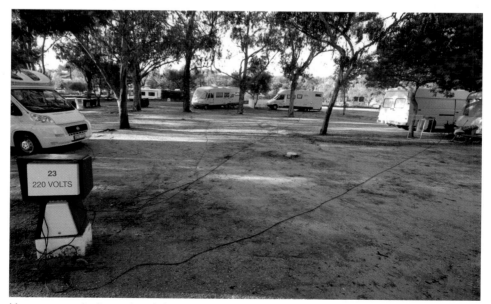

You may need a long electricity cable.

to reception to confirm the pitch location. En route to your pitch, fill up with water and empty the waste tanks if necessary. Set up on your pitch, level the camper, plug in to electricity checking polarity, turn on gas, and switch the fridge over from 12V to either gas or mains electricity.

You may think, as a paying guest, that providing level pitches is essential; strangely, many campsite owners do not consider it important. When stopping overnight it is not worth the effort rectifying a slight lean as long as you can sleep with your feet downhill and head uphill. We carry two levelling chocks and rarely use them; but if you intend to predominantly use campsites, then consider taking three or even four chocks. A simple, small two-way spirit level will give you an idea of how level the motorhome is as you jiggle around on the chosen spot. Invest in a chopping board with a drip edge to contain liquids when preparing food and ensure your plates have a raised edge, especially if you like gravy on your meal and not on your soft furnishings.

There are unwritten rules and etiquette that need to be followed at campsites to ensure you get on with your fellow campers and have a pleasant stay. Do not become a space-invader; people do not appreciate you cutting through the pitch they are paying for just because it is the quickest way to the toilet block. Having

Savaspace campsite pitch reservation sign.

used the washing-up sinks, wipe around the area and remove any food from the plug hole. After showering, mop up any water residue, soap and powder. Be aware of your noise; you may like the tune on the radio, but your neighbours might not. Marking your pitch whilst you go out for the day is common on campsites where customers are allowed to choose their own pitch. Tables and chairs are commonly left on pitch and some people use small signs such as those available from Savaspace (www.savaspace.co.uk, Tel: 07801 473047).

Some campsites, mainly in France, insist that swimming trunks, not shorts, are worn in swimming pools. Some Italian campsites insist on swimmers wearing hats. Charcoal barbecues are predominantly banned on Continental campsites. Some campsites prohibit the use of air conditioners and most ban generators.

Everyone looks cool around the pool in Italy.

Shower cubicles are often devoid of clothes hooks so people hang their clothes and towels over the top of the door. A bathrobe or dressing gown with a pocket for keys is useful. Even the best-maintained showers blocks look unclean after the morning and early evening rush hours, so it is worth taking some shower shoes with you. Any lightweight waterproof shoe or sandal will do as long as they prevent you coming in contact with the floor. Be warned, cheap flip-flops fling mud and dust up your damp legs as you walk back to your pitch. Very few campsite sinks have plugs, so you will need to have a universal plug in your wash kit.

Laundry day creates a small problem for motorhomers on tour because washing must not be strung up at Motorhome Stopovers or when Offsite-Parking as this constitutes camping and is forbidden. Whilst launderettes are available on the Continent, they can be difficult to find or park near. Self-service launderettes are beginning to appear in France at larger supermarket car parks. Most campsites have some sort of laundry system, from a service wash to hand washing sinks, and some have free hot water. Campsite washing machines are convenient to use, but are rarely cheap. Some campsites provide clothes spinners free of charge and using these significantly reduces drying times. If you intend to spend the majority of your time on a campsite with electricity, you may wish to buy a mini electric washing machine. These are available from Towsure (www.towsure.co.uk, Tel: 01142 503000) and other camping shops.

French supermarkets may have self-service launderettes.

Hand-turned worktop washing machines are available in Germany and we had a Wonder Wash when we were Full-Timing. Our Wonder Wash actually washed clothes and bedding well, and was fun to use. We especially liked that it was lightweight, cost-effective and could be used anywhere, water supply permitting. Perhaps the simplest and cheapest washing option is to acquire a large lidded bucket. Before you drive, load the bucket with washing, hot water and detergent and seal the lid. When you reach your destination the magic will have happened and your clothes will be clean, subject to rinsing. Line drying is quick and easy in warm climates, but it is worth packing items made from quick drying fabrics. During the summer there is no point packing two sets of bedding, just wash on a warm day. Few campsites forbid on pitch line drying and those that do normally provide a drying area. When offsite, or on inclement days, it is possible to use the motorhome bathroom as a drying room by opening the top vent and hanging clothes from the vent on clothes hangers, a carousel is ideal for smalls and swimming costumes. When electricity is available, open the bathroom door and aim a fan heater in.

Campsites are a great place to spring clean your motorhome, as everything can be placed outside during cleaning. People partial to crusty bread will soon discover that it is a motorhome nightmare. When cutting a French baguette crusty shards fire around the motorhome fixing in upholstery,

Spring cleaning the motorhome. Photo: Andy Glasgow.

curtains and bedding. Hence, many motorhomers opt to cut bread outside. Cleaning a vehicle inside and out is the surest way to find any wear and tear. Bored campers are sure to help you when you undertake repairs; they may also lend you tools and are sure to give you lots of 'useful' advice. There are plenty of accessory shops and garages across Europe should you need professional help or spares. French and German leisure vehicle dealers often have Motorhome Stopovers adjacent, so you can order and wait for spares and repairs. Repair jobs in Scandinavia are very expensive. If you plan to change the engine oil yourself whilst away, check that you can undo the sump plug because some require special tools. There are very few camping shops or motorhome dealers in Greece, so you may have to think around any issues. Water pumps, for instance, can be obtained from a boat or marine shop. *The Motorcaravan Manual* written by John Wickersham and published by Haynes is an essential guide for potential and current motorhome owners. The book discusses motorhome maintenance, including fixtures and fittings, gas, water, and electric systems. We recommend taking a copy if you are intending to undertake a long trip. You can buy a copy from Vicarious-Shop.com.

Naturist campsites, large and small, are located all across Europe. These sites are often in fantastic, secluded, and relaxing locations. You do not have to make a lifestyle choice to become a 'holiday naturist' and the experience is quite liberating. The Continentals are a lot more relaxed about naturism and it is possible to book into a naturist campsite without needing to be a member of a registered naturist organisation. Some campsites expect you to have a photographic naturist membership card, but some campsites issue temporary identification cards if you provide passport photos. Smaller naturist sites offer a rally-like feel and may organise communal meals and group activities. Naturism has a few simple rules: you do not have to be naked all the time – sometimes it is too cold, or you have had enough sun, or you are leaving the campsite. Generally nudism is only compulsory around the pool. You do have to be respectful of other people; no laughing, pointing, or taking photos unless you ask them to smile for the camera first. Contact British Naturism on www.bn.org.uk for more details.

Most campsites have small print in their terms and conditions stating they are not liable for items damaged or stolen from the campsite. Although rare, we receive reports of thefts from campsites every year. We recommend that you follow the same precautions as you would when Offsite-Parking: always lock up properly when leaving your pitch and do not leave anything unattended that you are not prepared to lose.

Designated motorhome parking in Plouarzel, France.

Motorhome Stopovers

Dedicated motorhome parking areas are provided in many European countries and these bring welcome tourists into well known and undiscovered areas alike. Motorhomers have over 8,000 Motorhome Stopovers to choose from and, as so many of them are free, it would be possible to tour Europe and never pay for camping or parking. Throughout this book we have referred to them as Motorhome Stopovers because overnight parking is normally allowed. Most Motorhome Stopovers also have a Service Point for water collection and disposal, but there are some service areas without parking. Motorhome Stopovers in rural locations normally offer free overnight parking and may charge €2-€3 for water. Motorhome Stopovers near the sea and at popular tourist destinations normally charge between €5-€20 for parking and may charge for water as well.

Motorhome Stopovers have a different name in every language:
- Aires de Service/Stationnement Camping Car – France and Belgium.
- Wohnmobil-Stellplätze – Germany, Austria, and Switzerland.
- Aree di Sosta – Italy.
- Bobil – Norway.
- Area de Servicio para Autocaravanas – Spain and Portugal.

Motorhome Stopovers had no established name in English until Vicarious Books published the *All the Aires* series of guidebooks. Aires is a shortened version of the French term Aire de Services, but even this is better described as

Motorhome Stopovers, like this one at Thann, allow motorhomers to come and go as they please.

serviced Motorhome Stopovers. To avoid confusion, the term Motorhome Stopover is used throughout this book except when discussing Motorhome Stopovers in specific countries, when the local term is sometimes used.

There is some confusion about motorway parking, especially in France where the motorway service stations are also referred to as Aires. The word 'aire' in French means 'area' and is used for lots of things. Anyone can stop at a motorway service station, but we receive more reports of theft at motorway service stations than any other place, especially in southern France and Spain. Local traffic police on the AP7 in Spain confirmed that vehicles, including motorhomes and trucks, were being broken into on that motorway. They believed it was a national problem on the Spanish motorway network. Therefore, we would never recommend that you park overnight at motorway service stations, even if they have a Service Point and what might appear to be suitable parking.

Aire simply means 'area' and this sign refers to motorway services. Motorhome Stopovers are occasionally signed 'Aire Camping-Car' and are usually indicated by a motorhome symbol.

Motorway parking areas may look suitable, but these are anonymous places and motorhomers should never park overnight on them.

AREA DE SERVICIOS PARA AUTOCARAVANAS

NORMAS DE UTILIZACIÓN DEL ÁREA PARA AUTOCARAVANAS

El estacionamiento máximo será de 48 horas.
- Queda prohibido sacar de la autocaravana cualquier elemento como sillas,mesas,barbacoas, toldo, tendal, etc... ya que esto es considerado como "acampada" y las leyes prohíben expresamente la acampada libre.
- El área debe de mantenerse en perfecto estado de limpieza.
- Cuando se use el borne de llenado y vaciado, no derramar líquidos fuera de la pileta y rejilla dejando todo limpio.
-"El punto de vaciado del WC está situado sobre la acera junto a las plazas de aparcamiento de disminuidos físicos"

RULES FOR THE CAMPERVAN AREA

Maximum parking 48 hours.
- Taking oug things such as chairs,tables, barbecues,awnings, etc... and hanging out clothes is FORBIDDEN because that is considered "camping" by   laws which expressly ban free camping.
- The area must be kept in perfect cleaning condition.
- When using the filling and emptying terminal, be careful not to spill liquids outside the sink and grille and leave everithing clean.
-"The point of emptying of theWC, is placed in the sidewalk, close to the parking for disable persons"

The law does not allow for camping equipment to be used at Motorhome Stopovers.

Municipally provided Motorhome Stopovers normally look like any other municipal parking area and you are free to come and go as you please. Guardians are only present at a small number of commercial Motorhome Stopovers, so for the most part there is no way of reserving a space. After your day out you should plan to visit two or three Motorhome Stopovers en route to your next chosen activity. If your first choice is full or unsuitable, move on to the next. You may be worried about using one for the first time. On your first attempt, visit in daylight to get a feel for it. On arrival, park, put the kettle on, and have a nice cup of tea. Look at the facilities, talk to the other motorhomers, and then look around the local area. By using Motorhome Stopovers you are likely to visit places not listed in any mainstream tourist information guidebook. When you find a relaxing or interesting place you can stay another day; if no time limit is displayed, then 48 hours is the unwritten rule. You should try to spend the equivalent of campsite fees locally in the village shops and cafés, or buy some diesel from the fuel station.

Motorhomes weighing up to 3,500kg are classified as cars in mainland Europe and, for safety reasons, car drivers are allowed to park and rest in their vehicles. This entitlement does not allow car drivers to put up tents or set up caravans because this is deemed camping. Owners of caravans and American-style fifth wheel caravans may think this unfair, but the rules are the rules and foreign tourists have no exemption. A motorhome is not deemed to be camping if it is self-sufficient; therefore the occupants can cook, eat, and sleep within the motorhome as long as they do not place anything outside. An onboard toilet is a necessity and waste water from sinks must not be discharged onto the ground or into containers that need to be placed outside. Some irresponsible motorhomers ignore these rules and use levelling chocks, put out tables and chairs, wind out awnings, hang up washing, run generators, and generally set up camp. Imagine how you would feel if people were doing that opposite your home. Presumably you would complain to your local council and demand that they banned motorhomes from the parking area.

Whatever country you are in, and regardless of what they are called, Motorhome Stopovers exist in four main forms:

Service Points: Service Points, sometimes referred to as bornes, dump or sani stations, are areas where motorhomes can dispose of waste water and toilet waste, refill drinking water tanks and sometimes hook-up to mains electricity. There are several manufacturers of self-contained Service Points

Go Motorhoming and Campervanning

Flot Bleu Service Point - France.

Euro Relais Mini - France and Portugal.

Urba Flux Service Point - France.

Holiday Clean - Germany and Norway. Photo: Andy Glasgow.

and the brand names include: Flot Bleu, Euro Relais, Aire Services and Holiday Clean. Approximately half of all the Service Points found around Europe are simply custom made by a builder and consist of a tap and a grated drain.

Service Points are normally attached to a motorhome parking area, but may be on the forecourt of a fuel station. Service Points are often turned off during winter to prevent frost damage, therefore you should plan to visit several Service Points during the day and service when you find one working.

Water: Unless there is a sign to say otherwise, it is safe to assume the water is potable, although tap hygiene is poor due to cross-contamination from toilet waste. Using disinfectant wipes or spray before drawing water from Service Points will improve hygiene. Taps vary widely; some are threaded to assist hose connection and

Use only water points marked as drinking water to fill your water tank, never to wash your toilet cassette. A bottle allows water refilling without the need for multiple hose adaptors.

others are too large to attach a hose. When payment is required to draw water it is normally limited to 100L.

Waste Water Disposal: Normally a drive-over metal grate is provided to facilitate the disposal of waste water. Badly chosen materials, poor or illogical construction and careless driving often lead to their destruction. Take a length of hosepipe to direct waste water accurately.

Never place the toilet nozzle around the tap, instead leave a gap of a few centimetres to avoid cross-contamination. The next person may use that tap for their fresh water.

Toilet Waste Disposal: Always wear waterproof gauntlets during toilet emptying. Take a moment to consider where and how to empty your toilet cassette, removing any grates before emptying. Do not rush cassette emptying as spillage and splashing will occur. Glugging can be reduced by pressing the vent button on the toilet cassette during emptying. Often a water tap is located above the toilet emptying point and these tend to flow even if payment is required for other services. Never put the cassette spout over a tap that may be used for drawing drinking water. We have a

Left: *Sometimes the toilet emptying point is covered by a grid.*
Right: *Having donned tough rubber gloves, lift the grid before emptying. This prevents solids and paper being left high and dry.*

Left: *Having emptied the toilet, flush the drain with your grey water or use the flushing system.*
Right: *Once the area is clean, replace the grid.*

gallery of photographs that show toilet waste sitting high and dry on drain covers. In most cases this is not because people have emptied the cassette in the wrong place, rather they have rinsed and emptied the cassette discharging leftover solids unexpectedly. Few Service Points are suitable for emptying fixed-tank toilet systems, such as those found on American RVs. We strongly recommend that you fit a macerator if your motorhome has a fixed toilet tank and travel with a long length of pipe.

Electric Hook-Up: Very few motorhome Service Points offer unlimited free electricity. Some of the professionally manufactured, self-contained Service Points require payment by coin or token before you can draw water and electricity. In this situation electricity is usually dispensed for a limited period, often one hour. The theory is that you can charge your batteries. In

This bollard provides a time-bound amount of electricity for a fee.

reality, this time is insufficient and few people bother to plug in. However, if you are organised you can charge all your battery-operated gadgets, blow-dry hair, boil kettles and fill flasks. Unfortunately, there is rarely an external trip switch on these Service Points and, once tripped, there is no way of making the electricity work again, despite having paid for it. Sometimes, particularly in Germany, a separate coin operated electricity bollard is provided and a time-bound or metered amount of electricity is available. Some stopovers include electricity in the nightly charge, but there may not be enough plug sockets for every motorhome. Stopping at a campsite is the only guaranteed way to get electricity.

Free electricity is uncommon at Motorhome Stopovers; when available, sharing is expected.

Custom Service Points vary widely as they are produced by local craftsmen.

Custom Service Points can be easy to miss.

Custom Service Points vary in usability.

Be responsible. If the Service Point is out of order, don't make the situation worse.

TURD: Totally Unbelievable Reckless Dumping.

Tokens And Pay Service Points:
Tokens are called '*jetons*' in French. Payment by credit card is increasing, and now less than one quarter of the Service Points in Europe require tokens.

Tokens are normally available from local shops, especially boulangeries (bakers), bar tabacs, tourist offices, the mairie (town hall) and campsites if adjacent. Tokens may be free, but typically cost €2-€3. Information panels or signs fixed to the Service Point normally indicate where tokens are available.

French tokens:

Techno Money (TM) has a distinctive pattern on the front. It is the same size as a 10p piece.

The 3/3 token is the same both sides with 3 grooves on each. It is the same size as a 10p piece.

The front of the Euro Relais (ER) token is branded. The token is slightly bigger than a 10p piece.

The 2/1 token has one groove on the front and 2 on the back. It is the size of a 2p piece.

The front of the Flot Bleu token is branded and the token is the size of a £1 coin, but not as thick.

Motorhome parking is normally indicated by a sign depicting a motorhome.

Overnight Parking: Motorhome parking is mostly municipally provided, but some privately-operated tourist attractions and supermarkets have a section of motorhome parking. Normally signs depicting a motorhome identify the area to be motorhome parking, although the signage does vary significantly. Sometimes designated parking areas are shared with cars and can be busy during the day, but empty at night. Motorhome Stopovers operate on a first come, first served basis and it is not possible to reserve a space. Stopping is generally limited to 48 hours, unless otherwise stated, because stopovers are designed to be used whilst touring and not for an extended holiday. Always park in designated bays, if provided, and never obstruct roadways or Service Points. Motorhome Stopovers may not have designated spaces, and it is normal to park less than a vehicle width from your neighbours. If you arrive at a stopover that is full, find another one. Twelve years ago motorhomes longer than 6m were rare, now motorhomes shorter than 6m are rare; the result is that a lot of the old parking areas are unsuitable for modern motorhomes. People with sub-6m motorhomes can take advantage of this and will find that they can stop on their own in wonderful locations. Anywhere that attracts a lot of motorhomes has had to manage the situation, and a lot of coastal towns have done this by banning motorhomes completely. Towns that have continued to accommodate motorhomes normally allow parking at specified places only, which are often barrier and parking meter controlled. To enjoy the freedom of motorhoming, we recommend that you plan your travels so that you avoid the obvious places. For example, if you want to drive around the French coast expect to pay at least €5 per night; you can get around this by heading inland each evening.

Vineyards, Farms And Private Gardens: Visiting a farm or vineyard where you can watch local producers at work, then park overnight is a romantic idea. Motorhomers are invited to do just this at 4,000 farms and vineyards across Europe. These are often available only to self-sufficient motorhomes because of the parking and camping rules previously discussed.

Farm stopover, France.

There are several membership schemes and publications to guide you. Vicarious Shop stocks guides for Denmark (*Nordic Camper Guide*), France (*France Passion*), Germany (*Bord Atlas*), and Italy (*Fattore Amico*). Apart from Denmark and Germany, these are motorhome-only membership schemes that allow 24 hours free parking at each listing. The local producers may wish to show you their wares, although there is no obligation to buy unless you are stopping at a restaurant or bar, and you are likely to be taken on an informative and interesting tour whether or not you can converse with your host. For the best experiences visit in summer and autumn. Remember, these places are at people's homes and businesses, so park as if you were on a Motorhome Stopover and do not set up camp.

In most European countries the legal level of alcohol in blood/breath when driving is significantly lower than the UK, and several European countries have zero percentage tolerance to alcohol on the breath. It is recommended that no alcohol is consumed if you intend to drive. Remember that alcohol consumed the night before may still be in the system, so leave plenty of time before driving.

Motorhome Campsites: There are certain areas that are overwhelmed by motorhomes. To accommodate them, local authorities have built what are best described as Motorhome Campsites. In fact, they are sophisticated Motorhome Stopovers, some of which have been developed by entrepreneurial individuals who have manipulated planning laws by only accommodating motorhomes. European motorhomers rarely use traditional campsites, despite this, they will pay to stop at Motorhome Campsites with reasonable prices. Motorhome Campsites differ from traditional campsites because they are mostly hardstanding, have no reception, and rarely have a sanitary block.

Motorhomers seem willing to use them because they are less expensive, are open all year, and accommodate only motorhomes. Electric hook-up is often available from pay meter points, and most people hook-up if it is reasonably priced. Credit card-operated barrier

PS : Des contrôles seront effectués

INFORMATION CAMPING - CARS

En raison des abus de certains camping-caristes, la commune va prochainement instaurer un droit de stationnement qui s'élèvera à 5 € par nuit.

Merci de votre compréhension.

Due to abuse of some camping car owners, the town will soon establish a parking fee that will be 5 € per night.

Thank you for undertanting.

Authorities at Catillon sur Sambre reacted to abuse by charging.

systems are becoming common at popular motorhoming destinations. Before entering you insert your credit or debit card, type in your vehicle registration number and the barrier opens. When you depart you insert your card and are charged accordingly. The barrier then opens and you are free to leave. Ironically, a few former municipal campsites have been converted into motorhome-only campsites and as a result are used all year round.

Using Motorhome Stopovers is a luxury not a right, so park sympathetically to your neighbours and use the Service Point and facilities responsibly. Always abide by the RESPONSIBLE rules:

R espect the environment
E lect to use un-crowded Motorhome Stopovers
S pend locally
P ark sensibly
O rganise your recycling
N o camping
S ave water
I mpeccable behaviour
B e quiet
L eave before you outstay your welcome
E valuate your impact

Service Points may have been broken by a previous visitor and may not be working.

Responsible use of Motorhome Stopovers is vital so that local communities keep them open. Use them, but don't abuse them. Common stopover abuse includes: not cleaning up the Service Point after emptying the toilet, camping on the stopover, parking over more than one bay, hanging out washing, breaking the Service Point, leaving without paying, and overstaying the time limit. It is with sadness that we have noticed the increase of these abuses over the past twelve years. Often Motorhome Stopovers are provided and funded by the local community, so make a conscious effort to repay their generosity. Remember, you represent the motorhome community; being miserly, abusing facilities and other unacceptable behaviour leads to resentment and stopovers closing.

You will stumble across Motorhome Stopovers in certain areas, but they may be as rare as hen's teeth ten miles down the road. To make the most of your trips you need to travel with the best information available. Motorhome Stopover guidebooks fall into two categories, those produced following professional inspection and those compiled from customer and tourist board submissions. When available, buy guidebooks that had professional inspectors gathering the information so that you have continuity of information. There are comprehensive stopover websites, including www.eurocampingcar.com and www.campingcar-infos.com. Read all the customer comments and make your own conclusions, also check the date of comments to ensure the information is current. Vicarious Media is a specialist publisher of Motorhome Stopover guides; visit www.Vicarious-Shop.com to see our full product range.

Overnight stopping place in Australia.

You may wish to Offsite Park beside the sea, but in reality most beach parking has overnight parking exclusion signs.

Offsite-Parking

Parking by the side of the road for a short period to rest is legally allowed in some European countries and can sometimes, especially in Scandinavia, be your only option. This has a few names, including 'free camping' and 'wild camping', however Offsite-Parking describes it better because that is essentially what you are doing. Scandinavia offers endless idyllic Offsite-Parking possibilities, but the opposite is true of the Mediterranean coast.

You can stay in some fantastic locations, but 90 per cent of your Offsite-Parking night stops will be unglamorous car parks and lay-bys. The terms 'free/wild camping' are misleading as they suggest that you unpack and set up as if on a campsite. In countries where stopping by the side of the road is legal, camping by the side of the road is not. When Offsite-Parking, the objective is to remain inconspicuous and be able to leave at a moment's notice. Always Offsite-Park considerately, trying to cause the least offence to locals. Remember Offsite-Parking is a luxury or a necessity, and should never be considered a right. This means that items should not be placed around the motorhome, such as tables, chairs and bikes, and if towing a trailer, it should remain hitched. Even if the law allows you to stop by the side of the road overnight, it does not allow you to stay there for long periods of time. You should aim to stop at teatime and depart after breakfast.

Do not set up camp when Offsite-Parking.

Scandinavia, with the exception of Denmark, encourages open access to its fantastic countryside and wilderness. The following phrases are often used to describe this idea: 'the freedom to roam', 'the right of public access', 'the right to roam', 'Everyman's Right'. Although described in many ways, this refers to the right to walk, cycle, ride, ski and camp on any land, or swim in any water body. Historically, open access was granted with walkers and canvas camping in mind and vehicles are prohibited from driving or parking off road. The scarcity of campsites in northern Scandinavia often makes Offsite-Parking the only option and the Scandinavian authorities are tolerant to this as long as you are parking on hardstanding. Taking advantage of this open access does not come without its responsibilities. The natives have great respect for their unique environments and protect them zealously. The rules are simple and must be obeyed:

- Do not disturb or destroy the environment.
- Dispose of your litter and waste only in the facilities provided.
- Private gardens and land under cultivation are exempted from open access.
- Camping or overnight parking is not permitted within 150m of a dwelling house.
- Local restrictions can apply, especially in nature reserves and in other protected areas.

Suitable parking places are hard to find in the populated southern parts of Scandinavia because of the 150m no-camping rule around dwellings. Always respect any local instructions; if you are willing to do that, then Scandinavia is waiting to be discovered.

Offsite-Parking is possible across most of Europe, although not necessarily legal. We have previously written that Offsite-Parking is not really an option at popular motorhome destinations, but once away from the masses you will have no problems if you choose locations wisely. The most important thing is to find somewhere that nobody has a strong feeling of ownership over, such as municipally provided parking outside sports facilities, and cemeteries often have deathly quiet parking. Bear in mind that out-of-town parking spots are often popular with local lovers or noisy youths and industrial estates become noisy around 4am. Do not park where it clearly signs not to and do not block driveways or entrances. When parking in idyllic locations, try to imagine how you would feel if you had paid a premium for a house with a view and a motorhome turned up and completely blocked it.

Most nights spent Offsite-Parking will be in urban car parks.

For your safety, and to ensure a restful night's sleep, park in an illuminated area close enough to habitation to feel safe, but far enough away to not cause offence. Always park so you can drive off at a moment's notice; face an exit and put everything away before you go to bed. Never put on external screens, use chocks or anything else that makes you exit the motorhome before you can drive off. Allow time to investigate your parking place, stop for a cup of tea or a meal and watch what and who is about. Have a walk around the area and familiarise yourself with it, and have a drink (not alcoholic) in the nearest bar so locals are not suspicious of you.

Do not Offsite-Park where signs prohibit.

When parking with other motorhomers, try to talk to your neighbours so they know who should be entering your motorhome. Do not drink because European law is tougher on drink drivers than UK law, and even one drink is too much. Once you've done all that, relax and enjoy the biggest freedom that motorhoming gives you: the ability to be at home wherever you are.

In areas where motorhomers are becoming a problem, the authorities may attempt to discourage them by moving them on. This is the first step before the barriers and exclusion signs go up. Being 'moved on' refers to being asked to leave by an official, often the

A motorhome fined for outstaying its welcome.

police. If you are 'knocked up', a knocking on the door, a reasonable response is that you are resting or that you are only parking overnight. Ensure you have stopped somewhere that you are legally allowed to, and even if you have, do not assume that you will not be disturbed. Normally, if you are knocked up by an official they will politely ask you to leave, but in the worst case scenario you may have to pay a fine. Police have fined motorhomers at popular Offsite-Parking spots in Spain and Portugal. On-the-spot fines for parking and traffic offences are common in Europe and immediate payment is expected.

Over the past twelve years we have noticed a dramatic increase in the number of height barriers and motorhome exclusion signs. The negative feelings towards motorhomers is generally created by bad motorhoming practices, such as emptying waste water tanks onto the ground, emptying toilets in any local drain regardless of its purpose, parking in huge numbers, running generators and being noisy, allowing pets to foul in the

Sign indicates motorhomes are not allowed to park between 8pm and 8am.

local areas, leaving litter, parking for the best view or to be closest to the beach, hanging out washing, and camping. Although your monthly budget can be reduced by Offsite-Parking, it is essential that this is done in a responsible manner and in accordance to the country's law regardless of what other motorhomers are doing. Failing to be responsible will just lead to more motorhome exclusion signs.

CHAPTER 7 - Key Country Guides

This chapter is a motorhomer's guide to the six countries you are most likely to visit. All the other countries of Europe are detailed on www.go-motorhoming.co.uk.

France

France has something for everyone from lavender days in Provence, to awesome alpine activities, to Mediterranean meanders. During the Tour de France, it appears that every motorhome ('*Camping Car*' in French) in France is lining the mountain stages. There are annual race stages through the Pyrénées and Alps, but the route changes every year. You can check the stages online at www.letour.fr.

Stenay, France.

Where To Stay

France has a mind-boggling 10,500 campsites that range from tiny summer-only camping areas to large family fun parks. The star rating system applied to French campsites is inconsistent, therefore we recommend that you walk around the campsite and check the facilities before you book in. French campsites are generally well signed from the nearest town or village, so you will not need directions to find them. Pleasant municipally run campsites are found all over France. Often they are located in small villages and normally alongside a river if there is one. The pitch fees are low and the facilities basic, but the campsites normally have a comfortable ambiance. Small rural campsites, with less than 25 pitches, are identified as *Aire Naturelle* in French. These small sites are often very basic but have a great appeal. Camping on farms is available through the *Bienvenue à la ferme* scheme, see www.bienvenue-a-la-ferme.com for details. Site entrances are clearly marked with the scheme's yellow-flower symbol. Les Castels is an organisation that promotes 40 campsites that are located in chateaux grounds, see www.camping-castels.co.uk for details. A good selection of campsites is listed at www.campingfrance.com. The French publication *Le Guide Officiel Camping Caravaning* lists 9,654 French campsites, including all the municipal and small campsites. This guide is written in French, but has an English key and is easy to use. Vicarious Shop stocks this guide and it is available to buy in large French supermarkets from April, but may not be restocked once sold out.

France has more than 3,000 Motorhome Stopovers called '*Aires de Services*', or Aires for short. These are detailed in *All the Aires France*, published by Vicarious Media. This is the only French Aires guide written in English and all 3,034 Aires listed have been inspected and photographed. *Le Guide National des Aires de Services* and *Le Guide Official Aires de Services* are produced by rival French motorhome magazines. The Aires are not inspected and few have photographs. The French language Aires guides are on sale in large French supermarkets from April, but may not be restocked once sold out. Members of France Passion can stop overnight for free in their motorhomes at farms and vineyards all over France. Membership runs from Easter to Easter and is gained by buying the current guidebook. Host establishments vary considerably so it is a good idea to check out two or three before deciding where to stop. This scheme gives you a unique insight into French culture and the hosts are likely to show you how the goods are produced and grown, even if language prevents conversation. GPS coordinates are supplied making remote host sites less difficult to find. Offsite-Parking is possible in France as long as it is undertaken in accordance with the traffic and parking laws.

Driving And Roads

France has twice the landmass of the UK, but has a similar number of residents. Consequently, traffic is light outside of major urban areas and there would be even less if all the motorways were free. French toll motorways are correctly named *autoroutes*, but are normally signed and referred to as *péage*, which translates to toll in English. These well-maintained motorways are quick and quiet but expensive, and for that reason most truck and domestic drivers use the non-toll main roads called *routes nationales*. Driving on French autoroutes is mind numbingly boring and it is hard to resist driving at high speeds, just to get it over with. Modern panel vans can easily drive at the 130kmh (80mph) upper speed limit and so can motorhomes if you are willing to accept the dramatically increased fuel consumption. Fuel at autoroute service areas is 10-20 cents per litre more than from supermarkets. Just in case you are only reading this section, for safety reasons never park overnight at autoroute service or rest areas and maintain vigilance when you use them at any time of day. For further information about autoroutes visit www.autoroutes.fr.

French trunk roads are called routes nationales. Often these main roads are marked red on road maps. Routes nationales are mostly single carriageway; despite this, they take the majority of traffic. The French driving style is consistent across the country. Mostly, car drivers are calm and unrushed in towns and villages, but they turn into speed-freaks on open roads. Truck drivers will maintain a speed of 90kmh (56mph) whenever possible. Due to a lack of passing places, frustrated drivers take extraordinary risks when overtaking, and being overtaken by trucks is very scary. Speeding is normal on the open road, but the 50kph (31mph) speed limit is observed in areas of habitation. In order to reduce accidents and speeding, more speed cameras are being installed, often they are not signed and may not be marked on maps. Mobile speed cameras and road checks are common at town and village boundaries. Bypasses are infrequent in France, so the main routes often pass through towns and villages. The majority of these main-road, built-up areas have a depressing look due to the grey film from pollution that coats the buildings. When driving past shops, be prepared for other drivers making emergency bread stops as they realise they just passed a bakery. See speed limits on page 214.

The nicest roads to drive are the lesser roads, marked yellow on the Michelin France road atlas. These minor routes tend to accommodate local traffic only. They pass through pretty landscapes and interesting villages, where you will be able to stop without disturbance.

Unfortunately, some French drivers seem to lack forethought and appear to be unable to assess how their actions will affect other road users. Head-on collisions, on perfectly straight roads, are common in France. Drivers often maintain their speed even if there is an obstruction on the road or their vehicle is sufficiently wide to overhang the white line. On narrow lanes, be prepared to pull off the road, avoiding any ditches, to allow oncoming vehicles to pass.

Priorité à Droite (priority to the right) is a tourist's worst nightmare. Thankfully, it has been removed from most towns and villages, but you are still likely to find yourself in a situation where you have no idea who has priority. What makes this inconsistency so dangerous is that some minor roads have priority over the main route and the local drivers will join the main route at speed. You should avoid giving way to vehicles on the right when it is not appropriate, doing so will cause all sorts of confusion, instead drive as if priority to the right exists unless road markings and signs prove otherwise. Some villages and towns have 'Priorité à Droite' signs written at the boundaries, but normally a sign displaying a yellow diamond indicates that there is no priority to the right. Cancellation signs will be displayed at village exits and normal road rules apply. Apparently, some villages are incapable of commitment and have removed all the road markings! At junctions where the priority is unclear, proceed

Priority to the right, France.

confidently but keep an eye on every direction. French drivers are very cautious at junctions and will willingly give way.

Roundabouts are a relatively new addition to French roads and help with priority issues. Most roundabouts flow the same as the UK, which may be indicated by signs saying '*Vous n'avez pas la priorité*' (no priority) or '*Cédez le passage*' (yield). Occasionally, in towns and villages the priority on a roundabout will be to the right; this is of course ludicrous, but no worse than putting traffic lights on roundabouts like they do in the UK. French traffic lights go from red to green skipping amber when releasing traffic and light changes tend to be a long time apart. Crossroads controlled by traffic lights may be left on flashing amber lights outside of rush hour, this indicates that you can proceed with caution; the problem is no one knows who has priority.

Roads are commonly marked with temporary '*Route Barrée*' signs (road closed) during road works or when markets are blocking the road. A deviation route is not always provided. Traffic calming chicanes and road humps are very common in towns and villages and their design ensures that you have to drive slowly over or around them to prevent damaging your vehicle.

When driving along narrow mountain lanes it is French driving etiquette to give-way to traffic travelling uphill, this includes pulling over and reversing if necessary. The French highway code requires the sounding of horns on twisting roads with reduced visibility. The Michelin France Tourist and Motoring Atlas highlights difficult or dangerous sections of roads. Less confident motorhome drivers should avoid these routes. High passes may be closed during winter and spring due to snow, snowdrifts, or wind. Never drive along roads signed 'Route Barrée' or 'Fermé', and never open gates that are used to close off mountain roads.

LPG availability varies from region to region but is sufficiently available across the whole country, especially on the autoroutes. LPG stations are listed in the rear of *All the Aires France* and on http://stations.gpl.online.fr/appli/index.php. www.jerouleaugpl.com/installateurs.php lists Total fuel stations with LPG.

Germany

Germany has it all: bountiful beer, amazing architecture, stunning scenery and toll-free roads. History vultures will be flying high at Hitler's Eagle's Nest. Bavaria has some pivotal pilgrimage sites including the *Wieskirche* and octagonal Chapel of Grace with its Black Madonna. Hopeless romantics may wish to start or end their scenic drive along *Romantische Strasse* taking in elaborate country houses and castles along the way. The Romantic Road is Germany's most popular tourist route and runs from Fussen in southern Bavaria 340km north to Wurzburg. Wine not meander alongside the Mosel or Rhine and marvel at the seemingly endless vineyards. Motorhome tourists are well catered for and can stop at any of the

Mosel Valley, Germany.

frequent *Stellplätze* along all three routes. Getting around by foot and bicycle could not be easier as the buses and ferries can transport you and your bike. Germany is crisscrossed by 7,000km of clearly signed cycle routes and there are plenty of marked walking trails as well. Germany's ski resorts are a well-kept secret. Generally the resorts are low-key, family-friendly, and affordable. Cash is king in Germany and very few places take credit or debit cards; consequently, you will have to make regular visits to cash machines.

Where To Stay
Germany has 3,500 campsites that cater for all desires and budgets. The German Tourist Board website lists 810 campsites, www.germany.travel/camping, and 2,056 German campsites are listed on http://en.camping.info/campsites.

Motorhome Stopovers are called *Wohnmobil Stellplätze* in Germany and there are nearly 4,000 to choose from. German motorhomers are happy to pay for electricity and plenty of Stellplätze offer hook-up. Often there will be meter-controlled hook-up bollards distributing electricity by kilowatts used or duration, commonly €2 for 12 hours. German Stellplätze are the best-kept Motorhome Stopovers in Europe, making Germany a joy to visit. There are several important road signs to watch out for: '*Nur Für*' means 'only for', '*Nur von*' means 'only from' whilst '*Frei*' means 'entry allowed' or 'parking spaces available'. The publication *Bord Atlas* by Reise Mobil, lists 2,382 Motorhome Stopovers and 1,096 farm and vineyard stops located in Germany. This comes as a pack of two guidebooks and is available from German bookshops and newsagents and from Vicarious Shop, www.Vicarious-Shop.com, Tel: 0131 208 3333. Offsite-parking is possible in Germany as long as it is undertaken in accordance with the traffic and parking laws.

Driving And Roads
Germany is a good driving country with only a few things to note. German driving tests are the most comprehensive in Europe and the driving style reflects this. Motorways, *Autobahn*, across Germany are toll free and frequently have only two lanes. Regardless of this there will be very fast cars on them. Some motorways have no speed limit, except during bad weather conditions when speed limits are indicated on overhead gantries. Vehicles over 3,500kg are frequently restricted to the inside lane, so look out for signs if you are affected. Do not 'middle lane' on German motorways because it is very dangerous, and you are likely to be

chastised. Before overtaking, take a good look in your mirrors, then if no speeding cars can be seen, indicate and overtake without delay. Motorway exits are signposted as '*Ausfahrt*'. Be aware that very short slip lanes followed by unbelievably steep bends are common.

Cyclists often have priority at traffic lights, therefore be vigilant when turning right in towns and be prepared to stop. Winter tyres are compulsory in Germany during snow or icy conditions, therefore you are advised to fit winter tyres if visiting between October and April. Snow chains should be used when needed or when indicated by signs. See www.bmv.de for detailed information about road rules. Free roadside parking may be time-bound and vehicles must display the arrival time on a time disc. Discs are available from newsagents for a few euros.

Low emission zones, called *Umweltzonen* in Germany, are on the increase. Vehicles entering an *Umweltzone* must display a colour-coded sticker (red, yellow, or green) that identifies the euro emission class of the vehicle. Non-compliance can result in a €40 fine. The sticker must be stuck on the inside of the windscreen at the bottom right corner. Some towns exclude higher emission, red stickered vehicles, and over time this will increasingly include yellow stickers. The sticker is valid for the entire life of the vehicle as long as the number plate is unchanged. Umweltzone stickers cost €29.90, see www.umwelt-plakette.de. Stickers can also be issued at local Dekra vehicle registration offices for €5. www.dekra.de has a Dekra station search facility. Just type in a postcode or town name and the details of the nearest Dekra office is displayed. Red stickers are awarded to Euro 2 and Euro 1 diesel cars/motorhomes with retrofit particulate filters. Yellow stickers are awarded to Euro 3 and Euro 2 diesel cars/motorhomes with retrofit particulate filters. Green stickers are awarded to Euro 4/5 and Euro 3 diesel cars/motorhomes with retrofit particulate filters. Green stickers are also awarded to cars/motorhomes with petrol engines fitted with closed-loop catalytic converters, excluding some older models. Visit www.umwelt.nrw.de and click 'English', then 'low emissions zones' for a good explanation of how engines are given a Euro rating. Also see page 37.

LPG is widely available and a list of LPG stations is provided at www.autogastanken.de/de/tanken/autogastankstellen-karte.html. The ADAC *Reise Atlas* (1:200,000) shows LPG stations and roads that exclude cars towing caravans. The atlas is available from bookshops in Germany and is updated biannually.

Italy

Rome was not built in a day and Italy has so much to see and do it is hard to know where to start. Italy has been a firm favourite with grand tourers

for centuries, and if we had only one month to travel Europe we would spend three weeks in Italy. Adventurous winter Sun-Seekers should head south to Sicily and drive around Etna, the largest volcano in Europe and one of the most active in the world. Visit www.funiviaetna.com for more information about visiting Etna.

Assisi, Italy. Photo: Andy Glasgow.

Where To Stay

Italian campsites are very expensive and you are unlikely to feel that you are getting good value for money. Poor facilities and unlevel pitches are common and you are advised to visit campsites that are in one of the discount schemes, see page 172. A database of Italian campsites is published online at www.camping.it. Look out for '*Agri Tourismo*' signs, as you will often be able to park overnight for a few euros.

Italy has approximately 2,700 Motorhome Stopovers called *Aree di Sosta*, which translates to area to stop. Motorhome Stopovers near tourist attractions are more like motorhome campsites; elsewhere they are located in municipal car parks and often have simple custom-built Service Points. There are few publications listing Italian stopovers. *Camperstop Europe* has a reasonable amount of Italian stopovers, but for definitive information you need the Italian guide *Aree de Sosta* by CamperLife, both guides are available at www.Vicarious-Shop.com. Details of Aree di Sostas can be found online at www.camperonline.it. Offsite-Parking is possible in Italy as long as the traffic and parking laws are complied with. Italians have an interesting take on what remote car parks should be used for, so bear this in mind when choosing overnight parking. Thankfully, the lovers tend to be quiet, but local youths will party late on Friday and Saturday nights. This can be a little alarming to start with, but you soon learn to sleep through it.

Driving And Roads

Whilst travelling south down Italy you will notice that road conditions continually deteriorate the further away from the industrial north you get. Motorways tend to have tolls, see www.autostrade.it, but the minor roads that run parallel are free and are often more interesting and challenging. Roads have been renumbered over the past few years, so maps and addresses may be out of date. Cycling clubs are common and pelotons snake their way along minor roads on Sundays. Road drainage appears uncommon in southern Italy, so avoid driving during rain. Road signage can be difficult to interpret so take some time to get it right. For example, a straight on sign often looks to be indicating left or right. If you need to stop and think about which way to go, putting your hazard lights on will be enough to encourage people to drive around you. The south of Italy is less busy than the north, but Italians love their cars so there is always some traffic. Appalling congestion occurs after supper because everybody with a car cruises around town, so try to avoid driving between 7pm and 10pm. Perhaps the recession will encourage them to promenade instead.

There are rumours that the Italians are mad drivers with one hand always on the horn. OK, they are expressive with their horns, but it is an unofficial language that is easy to learn. One short beep from a following car is a warning that they are overtaking or simply 'I am here'. Two beeps means 'ciao' and they are generally saying hello to someone they know. A progression of beeps or one long beeeeeeeep usually means you or something else is in the way; either they have nearly driven into you or there is a parked car blocking the route. Italians drive at two speeds, fast and slow. People driving slowly are happy to drift along and are not concerned by confused tourists. People in a hurry will drive with full beam lights on and will flash manically; as a general rule everyone gets out of their way.

Parking is an Italian sport and any space is fair game, even if it blocks the road. When confronted by a blocked road it is standard practice to give a long horn blast, shopkeepers and passersby soon inspect the situation then summon the owner to move the vehicle. Many cities do not allow tourist traffic through the historic centre, so park on the outskirts and use public transport to get in. Tailgating is something you have to accept.

Some ski resorts can only be accessed by crossing high mountain passes that are prone to blockages after light snow and wind. All tourist offices receive daily updates about mountain-pass conditions and a three-day snow forecast. Winter tyres are required between 15th October and 15th April.

If you have a bike rack or anything that protrudes from the rear of your motorhome, ensure you identify it with a hazard warning sign. These are 50cm square with red and white reflective stripes.

 LPG is widely available. Fuel stations may discount fuel prices at weekends, and self-service pumps are marked '*Fai Dante*' and are often five per cent cheaper.

Portugal
Portugal has a relaxed pace of life that follows the seasons. Agricultural vehicles of all types are used as daily transport, testament to the family farm lifestyle so prevalent in the interior. During winter the Atlantic coast is often windier and wetter than the more sheltered Algarve; unsurprisingly, this is where most motorhomes congregate. If you drive north, away from the Sun-Seekers, you will find the wetlands around Aveiro. This area provides shellfish for birds and fishermen alike who navigate the creeks in traditional colourful fishing boats.

São Jacinto, Portugal.

Where To Stay
Portugal has approximately 300 campsites, many of which are open all year. 140 campsites are listed on www.campingportugal.org and 160 are listed on www.visitportugal.com. The publication *Roteiro Campista* (Camping Portugal) details 238 Portuguese campsites. This guidebook is available from tourist offices in Portugal.

 There are over 100 Motorhome Stopovers listed in *All the Aires Spain and Portugal*. Offsite-Parking is possible, but 'No Motorhome' signs and restrictions are common along the coast.

Driving And Roads

Compared to Spanish roads, Portuguese roads are in poor condition and country lanes are very bumpy. Main roads are busy and the surface has often deteriorated and is potholed. The local driving style is calm, and the local roads are quiet. Portuguese toll roads have a 12-hour time restriction. As always, for safety reasons do not park overnight at motorway rest areas, but in this case, time is also against you. Electronic tolls, signed '*Lanco Com Portagem*', apply on many of the formerly free stretches of motorway. This is an automated system and there are no tollbooths. Instead, an electronic device has to be leased or a three-day ticket can be purchased. These are available from motorway service stations and at borders and must be acquired before you use the motorways. Visit www.tollcard.pt or see the tourist board website, www.visitportugal.com.

LPG is available in Portugal at many fuel stations, www.autogas.pt. Fuel is 10 cents more per litre in Portugal than it is in Spain.

Spain

Southern coastal Spain provides the warmest winter temperatures in mainland Europe, thus motorhome and caravan users migrate there from all over the Continent. The warm winters make it viable to grow a wide selection of fruits, vegetables, and salad crops. The evidence of this intensive production is clearly visible as thousands of hectares of southern Spain are cloaked in plastic. To experience a quieter and more beautiful Spain, drive inland across the mountain plains.

View from N340, Spain.

Go Motorhoming and Campervanning

Where To Stay

Spain has 1,200 campsites. There are many large campsites located along the southeastern coast that are suitable for long-term winter holidays. Rallies are held at these campsites by motorhome and caravan clubs from all over Europe. The publication *Guia Camping* details campsites in Spain and Portugal and has a searchable database of campsites on the supporting website, www.guiacampingfecc.com.

There are 300 Motorhome Stopovers in Spain. Almost half are located above Portugal, between the Atlantic coast and San Sebastián. Most inland stopovers are underused despite being free and open all year. Full details are provided in *All the Aires Spain and Portugal* available from www.Vicarious-Shop.com. If you dream of driving slowly down the Spanish Mediterranean coast and stopping wherever takes your fancy, you are going to be disappointed. Offsite-Parking is nearly non-existent as more and more motorhome exclusion signs are erected, and you are unlikely to find a free Motorhome Stopover near the sea.

Unfortunately, there is an element of crime targeted at tourists. Many campsites display warning and disclaimer notices about leaving belongings outside and valuables on display when you are away from your pitch. Spanish highway police on the AP7 confirmed that break-ins both on trucks and motorhomes were a real problem at motorway rest areas, but rarely occur off the motorway network. Do not stop overnight at motorway service or rest areas and be vigilant at all times when visiting them.

Driving And Roads

In general, Spanish roads are the best in Europe having recently been subject to an extensive EU road improvement programme. Although this has made Spanish roads easy and pleasant to drive on, it can cause navigation issues for both humans and satellite machines. Ensure you have up-to-date mapping with you. Away from major cities the local driving style is generally non-aggressive, cautious, and very tolerant. Toll roads along the east coast connect the popular coastal resorts. There are also reasonable free roads that follow the same route. This coast is very busy and is virtually all built-up. Driving the central route up or down is quiet, beautiful and toll free.

Speed detectors linked to traffic lights are common at town boundaries. The traffic lights stop speeding vehicles before they enter the built up areas. Spanish road planners have adopted a type of junction which would be a roundabout elsewhere in Europe. To prevent vehicles turning left across the traffic a right-hand slipway sweeps away and back at right angles to the road. Drivers then have to give way to traffic on both carriageways. This type of junction is likely to be traffic light controlled in towns. These junctions can be unexpected so look out for them!

Almost a roundabout in Spain.

 LPG has limited availability, see www.repsolypf.com and www.aoglp.com. The majority of Spanish LPG outlets are detailed in *All the Aires Spain and Portugal*.

United Kingdom

The UK is probably the most diverse country in Europe and there is so much to see and do that a lifetime of weekends and holidays can easily be filled. Visiting country houses and historical industrial buildings will give you a good understanding of how the people that shaped the UK's countryside and industry lived. Members of the National Trust, www.nationaltrust.org.uk, and English Heritage, www.english-heritage.org.uk, have free access to hundreds of historic buildings and places of interest. You can join at one of the more popular sites so there is no need to take out membership in advance. National Trust members also have access to buildings owned by the National Trust for Scotland, www.nts.org.uk. The National Trust offers free entry to members of affiliated overseas National Trusts, so bring your membership card if you are a member in: Australia, Canada, Guernsey, Isle of Man, Italy, Jersey, Malta, or New Zealand. Camping is practical all year in England and Wales because of the

Thorpeness, Suffolk.

mild climate, but it is best to tour from April to October to avoid dreary winter weather and cold spells. Cornwall, Ireland and Wales are the wettest regions of the UK. Scotland is a bit too cold for winter camping, so plan a summer visit. Be warned, mosquitoes are a problem.

Where To Stay

There are 2,400 campsites in the UK and a wide network of independent campsites are detailed in numerous campsite guides available from www.Vicarious-Shop.com. There are several UK campsite directories online. Unfortunately, the UK does not have a network of Motorhome Stopovers, but does have about 4,000 mini camping farm sites with pitch fees as low as £3.50 per night. The easy way to gain access to these mini camping sites is to join one of the camping clubs. The Camping and Caravanning Club allows caravans, motorhomes and tents on its campsites, see www.campingandcaravanningclub.co.uk, Tel: 02476 475442. Membership gives access to over 100 club sites and more than 1,600 certified sites (mini camping). Many of the larger club sites are open to non-member visitors, who pay the full rate. Annual membership costs from £37 and temporary three-month membership is available to foreign nationals for about £20. Membership can be taken out at club sites. Members of The Caravan Club can camp in caravans and motorhomes at over 200 club sites, including Crystal Palace in London, and 2,500 small Certified Locations (mini camping). Annual membership costs £46 and it is possible to join at any club site. See www.caravanclub.co.uk, Tel: 01342 326944.

Certified Locations/Sites (CL/CS) are restricted to a maximum of five member caravans/motorhomes per night. These sites are located at farms, pubs and in people's gardens, so you are able to experience true UK culture in otherwise inaccessible areas. Every site offers water and a waste disposal facility, some offer electricity and showers. Information about these locations is provided in the clubs' handbooks and on their websites.

There are so few official Motorhome Stopovers in the UK that you could publish information about them on two sides of A4 paper. Visit www.ukmotorhomes.net for a current list. Over 500 pubs allow members of a UK scheme called Motorhome Stopovers to stop for the night. Membership costs £30 per year and members have access to the pub database on www.motorhomestopover.co.uk. There is another UK scheme called Brit Stops that emulates France Passion, see www.britstops.com for details. Although by-laws generally exclude Offsite-Parking, in practice, it is possible to Offsite-Park in the UK if you stop late and leave early, but avoid the obvious tourist hot spots and the coast. Pub landlords and farmers will often let you stop for the night if asked nicely. Some Scottish Islands allow Offsite-Parking, but check with the local tourist office first.

Driving And Roads

Remember to drive on the left. Britain has some of the busiest roads in Europe and most towns in the Southeast and the Midlands experience rush hour congestion from 8am-9am and 5pm-6pm. Rural counties experience less congestion. The M25 around London can come to a standstill at any time as can the toll-free M6 near Birmingham. Despite local opinion, the roads in the UK are good and most are free to use, apart from toll bridges crossing major estuaries and the M6 toll road around Birmingham.

There are about 2,000 low bridges in the UK. Bridge heights and road widths are often shown only in feet and inches, not metres. Make sure you convert your vehicle's measurements into feet and keep it on display in the cab. Truckers' maps, showing bridge heights, are available at service stations. Country lanes are narrow and often two-way. Roads in the West Country and Wales can be very narrow and busy during the tourist season; be prepared to use the pull-ins provided or reverse if necessary. London has both a low emission zone, www.tfl.gov.uk/lezlondon, and a congestion charge, www.tfl.gov.uk/roadusers/congestioncharging. There is no need to drive through London and it is easier, and probably cheaper, to stay overnight outside of the zones and use public transport to get in.

LPG is available in the UK, but not from every fuel station. A map of LPG stations is displayed at www.drivelpg.co.uk/map/index.php.

The Crown Dependencies Of Jersey, Guernsey And The Isle Of Man

There are three Crown Dependency islands: Jersey, Guernsey, and the Isle of Man, none of these islands is part of the EU. Jersey and Guernsey are located off the coast of France. Motorhomes are accepted as long as campsites are pre-booked. Sea crossings must be made with Condor Ferries and motorhomes cannot exceed 7m in length. More information can be found at www.visitguernsey.com and www.jersey.com. The Isle of Man is located between Ireland and Wales and is accessible via ferry from both the UK and Ireland. There are 19 campsites listed on the tourist board website, www.visitisleofman.com.

Europe-Wide Additional Information

Country	EU Member	Schengen Zone	Currency	Emergency Phone Numbers Dial 112 Europe-Wide (English spoken)	Tourist Information
Albania	X	X	Lek	Dial 129 for Police, 128 for Fire Service, 127 for Ambulance (taxis may be quicker!)	www.albania.al
Andorra	X	X	Euro	Dial 110 for Police, 112 for general emergencies, 116 for medical emergencies, 118 for Ambulance/Fire Service	www.andorra.ad
Austria	Y	Y	Euro	Dial 112 for all emergencies	www.austria.info/uk
Belarus	X	X	Ruble	Dial 102 for Police, 101 for Fire Service, 103 for Ambulance	http://eng.belarustourism.by
Belgium	Y	Y	Euro	Dial 112 for all emergencies	www.belgiumtheplaceto.be (Wallonia), www.visitflanders.co.uk (Flanders)
Bosnia and Herzegovina	X	X	Konvertibilna Marka	Dial 122 for Police, 123 for Fire Service, 124 for Ambulance	http://www.bhtourism.ba/
Bulgaria	Y	X	Lev	Dial 112 for all emergencies	www.bulgariatravel.org or www.travel-bulgaria.com
Croatia	Y	X	Kuna	Dial 112 for all emergencies	www.croatia.hr
Czech Republic	Y	Y	Koruna (Crown)	Dial 158 for Police, 150 for Fire Service, 155 for Ambulance	www.czechtourism.com
Denmark	Y	Y	Krone (DKK)	Dial 114 for Police, 112 for Ambulance	www.visitdenmark.com
Estonia	Y	Y	Euro	Dial 110 for Police, 112 for Fire Sevice and Ambulance	www.visitestonia.com or www.tourism.ee
Finland	Y	Y	Euro	Dial 112 for all emergencies	www.visitfinland.com
France	Y	Y	Euro	Dial 17 for Police, 18 for Fire Service, 15 for medical emergencies, 112 for all emergencies	http://int.rendezvousenfrance.com or www.france.fr
Germany	Y	Y	Euro	Dial 112 for all emergencies	www.germany-tourism.co.uk
Greece	Y	Y	Euro	Dial 100 for Police, 166 for Ambulance, 112 in an emergency	www.visitgreece.gr Tel: 020 7495 9300
Hungary	Y	Y	Forint	Dial 112 for all emergencies	htpp://gotohungary.com
Iceland	X	Y	Krona	Dial 444 1000 for Police, 1770 for medical emergencies 112 for all emergencies	www.visiticeland.com
Ireland	Y	X	Euro	Dial 112 for all emergencies	www.ireland.ie or www.discoverireland.com
Italy	Y	Y	Euro	Dial 112 for all emergencies	www.visititaly.com
Kosovo	X	X	Euro	Dial (1')92 for Police, (1)93 for Fire Service, (1)94 for Ambulance (*add 1 from a mobile)	http://kosovotourismcenter.com or http://beinkosovo.com

Country		Currency	Emergency numbers	Website
Latvia	Y	Y	Euro	Dial 112 for all emergencies	www.latvia.travel
Lithuania	Y	Y	Euro	Dial 112 for all emergencies	www.lietuva.lt
Luxembourg	Y	Y	Euro	Dial 113 for Police, 112 for all emergencies	www.visitluxembourg.lu
Macedonia (Republic of)	X	X	Denar	Dial 192 for Police, 193 for Fire Service, 194 for medical emergencies	www.exploringmacedonia.com or http://travel2macedonia.com.mk
Malta	Y	Y	Euro	Dial 112 for all emergencies	www.visitmalta.com
Montenegro (Republic of)	X	X	Euro	Dial 122 for Police, 123 for Fire Service, 124 for Ambulance, 112 for all emergencies	www.visit-montenegro.com
Morocco	X	X	Dirham	Dial 19 for Police, 15 for Fire Service, 15 for Ambulance (taxis may be quicker!)	www.visitmorocco.com or www.morocco.com
Netherlands	Y	Y	Euro	Dial 112 for all emergencies	http://netherlands-tourism.com or www.visitholland.nl
Norway	X	Y	Kroner (NOK)	Dial 112 for Police, 110 for Fire Service, 113 for Ambulance	www.visitnorway.com
Poland	Y	Y	Zloty	Dial 997 for Police, 998 for Fire Service, 999 for Ambulance	www.poland.travel
Portugal	Y	Y	Euro	Dial 112 for all emergencies	www.visitportugal.com
Romania	Y	X	Leu	Dial 112 for all emergencies	www.romaniatourism.com
Russian Federation	X	X	Ruble	Dial 112 for all emergencies	www.visitrussia.org.uk
Serbia (Republic of)	X	X	Dinar	Dial 192 for Police, 193 for Fire Service, 194 for Ambulance	www.serbia.travel
Slovakia	Y	Y	Euro	Dial 158 for Police, 112 for all emergencies	www.slovakia.org
Slovenia	Y	Y	Euro	Dial 113 for Police, 112 for all emergencies	www.slovenia.info
Spain	Y	Y	Euro	Dial 112 for all emergencies	www.spain.info
Sweden	Y	Y	Krona	Dial 112 for all emergencies	www.visitsweden.com
Switzerland	X	Y	Swiss franc	Dial 117 for Police, 118 for Fire Service, 144 for Ambulance, 1414 for Swiss Rescue	www.myswitzerland.com
Turkey	X	X	Lira	Dial 155 for Police, 110 for Fire Service, 112 for Ambulance	www.gototurkey.co.uk
Ukraine	X	X	Hryvnia	Dial 102 for Police, 101 for Fire Service, 103 for Ambulance, 112 for all emergencies	www.traveltoukraine.org
United Kingdom	Y	X	Pound (Sterling)	Dial 999 or 112 for all emergencies	www.visitbritain.com

European Driving Speed Limits and Regulations by Vehicle Weight for Motorhomes and Caravans

European Country	MAM (Maximum Authorised Weight of Tow Vehicle or Motorhome)	Built-up Areas (Cities, Towns, Villages)	Single Carriageways, Lanes, Trunk Routes, Bypasses, Single-Track Roads, Highways	Dual Carriageways, Expressways	Motorways, Autoroutes, Autobahn, Autostrada	Trailer, Caravan, A-frame Restrictions	Other Speed and Weight Restrictions in Europe
Andorra	-	50kmh	60kmh	90kmh	-		
Austria	<3,500kg	50kmh	100kmh	-	130kmh	80kmh (trailer >750kg) and 100kmh (trailer <750kg)	
	>3,500kg	-	70kmh	-	80kmh	-	GO-Box required, see www.go-maut.at
Belarus	-	60kmh	90kmh	-	120kmh	-	
Belgium	<3,500kg	50kmh	90kmh	-	120kmh	-	Vehicles >3500kg cannot drive in left lane on roads with 3+ lanes
	>3,500kg	50kmh	90kmh	-	90kmh	-	60kmh on highways for vehicles >7.5 tons
Bosnia and Herzegovina	-	50kmh	80kmh	-	130kmh	-	
Bulgaria	<3,500kg	50kmh	90kmh	-	130kmh	70kmh (S) and 90kmh (M)	
	>3,500kg	50kmh	80kmh	100kmh	100kmh	70kmh (S) and 90kmh (M)	
Croatia	<3,500kg	50kmh	80kmh	-	100kmh	80kmh (S) and 90kmh (M)	
	>3,500kg	50kmh	80kmh	-	90kmh	-	
Cyprus	-	50kmh	80kmh	-	100kmh	-	
Czech Republic	<3,500kg	50kmh	80kmh	90kmh	130kmh	80kmh (S) and (M)	
	>3,500kg	50kmh	80kmh	-	80kmh	-	
Denmark	<3,500kg	50kmh	80kmh	90kmh	130kmh	70kmh (S) and 80kmh (M)	
	>3,500kg	50kmh	70kmh	-	80kmh	-	
Estonia	-	50kmh	90kmh	110kmh (summer)	90kmh	-	
Finland	<3,500kg	50kmh	-	80kmh	120kmh	80kmh (S) and (M)	Motorway speed limits are always displayed by traffic signs, between 80kmh-120kmh
	>3,500kg	50kmh	80kmh	-	80kmh	-	60kmh on highways for vehicles >7.5 tons

< = Less than; > = More than. (S) = Single Carriageway. (M) = Motorway.

*Higher speed limit applies to trailers/caravans with braking systems. Lower speed applies to trailers/caravans, without braking systems.

Country	Weight						Notes
France	<3,500kg	50kmh	90kmh	110kmh	130kmh	-	
	>3,500kg	50kmh	80kmh	80kmh	90kmh	80kmh	
Germany	<3,500kg	50kmh	100kmh	-	130kmh	80kmh	The standard speed limit applies unless stated otherwise on traffic signs
	>3,500kg <7500kg	50kmh	80kmh	-	80kmh	60kmh	
	>7,500kg	50kmh	60kmh	-	80kmh	60kmh	
Gibraltar	-	31mph (50)	-	-	-	-	
Greece	<3,500kg	50kmh	90kmh	110kmh	130kmh	80kmh	
	>3,500kg	50kmh	80kmh	80kmh	85kmh	80kmh	
Hungary	<3,500kg	50kmh	90kmh	110kmh	130kmh	70kmh (S) and 80kmh (M)	
	>3,500kg	50kmh	70kmh	-	80kmh	-	
Iceland	-	50kmh	80kmh	-	90kmh	-	Highways are defined as gravel roads and motorways as asphalt roads.
Ireland	<3,500kg	50kmh	100kmh	-	120kmh	80kmh	
	>3,500kg	50kmh	80kmh	-	90kmh	-	
Italy	<3,500kg	50kmh	90kmh	110kmh	130kmh	70kmh (S) and 80kmh (M)	
	>3,500kg	50kmh	80kmh	-	100kmh	-	
Latvia	<7,500kg	50kmh	90kmh	90kmh	90kmh	-	
	>7,500kg	50kmh	80kmh	80kmh	80kmh	-	
Lithuania	<3,500kg	50kmh	90kmh	-	130kmh	90kmh	Roads without asphalt are limited to 70kmh. Reduced speed limits all roads Nov-Mar
	>3,500kg	50kmh	80kmh	-	90kmh	-	
Luxembourg	<3,500kg	50kmh	90kmh	-	130kmh	75kmh (S) and 90kmh (M)	
	>3,500kg	60kmh	75kmh	-	90kmh	-	
Macedonia (Rep)	-	60kmh	80kmh	100kmh	120kmh	-	
Montenegro (Rep)	-	50kmh	80kmh	-	100kmh	-	
Netherlands	<3,500kg	50kmh	80kmh	100kmh	120kmh	80kmh (S) and 90kmh (M)	
	>3,500kg	50kmh	80kmh	80kmh	80kmh	-	
Norway	<3,500kg	50kmh	80kmh	90kmh	100kmh	60kmh or 80kmh*	Vehicles towing caravans must be equipped with special rear view mirrors
	>3,500kg	50kmh	80kmh	-	80kmh	-	

Continued overleaf

Go Motorhoming and Campervanning

European Country	MAM (Maximum Authorised Weight of Tow Vehicle or Motorhome)	Built-up Areas (Cities, Towns, Villages)	Single Carriageways, Lanes, Trunk Routes, Bypasses, Single-Track Roads, Highways	Dual Carriageways, Expressways	Motorways, Autoroutes, Autobahn, Autostrada	Trailer, Caravan, A-frame Restrictions	Other Speed and Weight Restrictions in Europe
Poland	<3,500kg	50kmh	90kmh	100kmh	140kmh	70kmh (S) and 80kmh (M)	
	>3,500kg	50kmh	70kmh	80kmh	80kmh	-	
Portugal	<3,500kg	50kmh	90kmh	100kmh	140kmh	-20kmh	
	>3,500kg	50kmh	80kmh	80kmh	90kmh	-	
Romania	<3,500kg	50kmh	90kmh	100kmh	130kmh	-10kmh	
	>3,500kg	50kmh	80kmh	90kmh	110kmh	-	
Russian Fed.	-	60kmh	90kmh	-	110kmh	-	
Serbia/ Montenegro	<3,500kg	50kmh	100kmh	-	120kmh	-	
	>3,500kg	50kmh	80kmh	-	80kmh	-	
Slovakia	<3,500kg	50kmh	90kmh	-	130kmh	90kmh	
	>3,500kg <6,000kg	50kmh	90kmh	-	90kmh	-	
Slovenia	<3,500kg	50kmh	90kmh	110kmh	130kmh	100kmh	
	>3,500kg	50kmh	80kmh	80kmh	90kmh	-	
Spain	Motorhomes <3,500kg	50kmh	70kmh	80kmh	90kmh	70kmh (S) and 80kmh (M)	
	Motorhomes >3,500kg	50kmh	70kmh	80kmh	80kmh	-	
Sweden	<3,500kg	50kmh	70kmh	100kmh	110kmh	50kmh or 80kmh*	
	>3,500kg	50kmh	70kmh	-	90kmh	-	
Switzerland	<3,500kg	50kmh	80kmh	100kmh	120kmh	80kmh	Towing cars on motorways is only permitted up to the next exit at a maximum speed of 40kmh.
	>3,500kg	50kmh	80kmh	80kmh	80kmh		
Turkey	-	50kmh	90kmh	-	120kmh	-10kmh	
Ukraine	-	60kmh	90kmh	110kmh	130kmh	-	
United Kingdom	<3,050kg unladen weight	30mph (48)	60mph (96)	70mph (112)	70mph (112)	50mph (80) (S), 60mph (96) (D+M)	No trailers in the right-hand lane of a motorway with three or more lanes.
	>3,050kg unladen weight	30mph (48)	50mph (80)	60mph (96)	70mph (112)	60mph (96) (D+M)	

< = Less than; > = More than. (S) = Single Carriageway. (M) = Motorway.

*Higher speed limit applies to trailers/caravans with braking systems. Lower speed applies to trailers/caravans, without braking systems.

Please make sure up to date on local laws and driving regulations before travelling to any foreign country and always adhere to road signs while driving abroad.

Now that you are an armchair expert, you are ready to take the next step with confidence. If you already own a motorhome, book a crossing, pack your guidebooks, then go and enjoy the freedom of motorhoming. Motorhome virgins should rent or buy something affordable that is a manageable size.

Remember that a motorhome is not a pet and can be just for Christmas. As we explained, the perfect motorhome does not exist. During your first few trips, you discover whether you are willing to compromise accessibility and manoeuvrability over living space.

Before you depart, make sure that you have packed the essential items listed in Chapter 2. For now, ignore any must-have gadgets and gizmos and reconsider them once you have cut your teeth. Make sure your administration is in order and fit a safe so that you can keep your passports, important documents, and valuables under lock and key. Ensure that you pack enough of your favourite teabags to last your trip; spices are also hard to find on the Continent. Remember to weigh your motorhome once everything is packed.

We have explained what to expect from the different accommodation options and you know how to be a responsible motorhome tourist. We recommend that you sample everything that is on offer so that you can find out for yourself what type of motorhomer you are. Use the country guides to help you decide where to go and explore.

Chris's top tip: Buy a motorhome no longer than 6m that weighs no more than 3,500kg.

Meli's top tip: Don't worry about the destination, simply plan your trips around the things you want to see and do.

Vicarious Media's top tip: Knowledge is power and ignorance is avoidable, so pack your maps, tourist, hobby, and stopover guidebooks before you depart.

Vicarious Cat's top tip: Don't forget your dogs and cats need a PETS passport.

Updates and amendments to this book are provided on www.go-motorhoming.co.uk. We welcome your comments, experiences and updates.

Aire in sunny quarry near tourist attractions. Fontville, France.

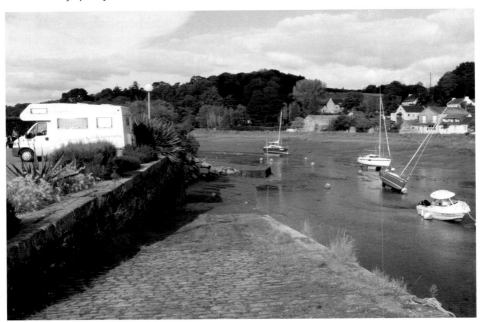

Taulé Aire along the Penzé river, France.

A

B

F